AMUSEMENT

A

Force in Christian Training.

AMUSEMENT

A

FORCE IN CHRISTIAN TRAINING.

Four Discourses

BY THE

REV. MARVIN R. VINCENT,

Pastor of the First Presbyterian Church, Troy, N. Y.

TROY, N. Y.:

WM. H. YOUNG, 8 & 9 FIRST STREET.

1867.

MUNSELL, PRINTER, ALBANY.

These discourses are not presented as a series. With the exception of the last, which was prepared merely for publication, they were delivered at considerable intervals, and to meet certain aspects of the subject as they presented themselves. As they all develop substantially the same principles, they will probably contain some repetitions. The interest awakened by the publication of the essay before the Albany Convention, and the very general desire expressed to see the second and third of these discourses in print, have decided the author against remoulding the whole into one treatise which he at one time contemplated. He therefore sends them forth in their original shape, with earnest prayer that the great Head of the church may use them, with all their imperfections, to awaken Christian thought and friendly discussion on a subject of vital importance to the welfare of our youth.

MARVIN R. VINCENT.

TROY, *Jan. 9th*, 1867.

RELIGION AND AMUSEMENT.

AN ESSAY,

DELIVERED AT THE

INTERNATIONAL CONVENTION OF YOUNG MEN'S CHRISTIAN ASSOCIATIONS,

HELD IN

ALBANY, JUNE 1, 1866,

RELIGION AND AMUSEMENT.

The religious thought of the age must soon face this subject more fairly than it has yet done; and seek for some more satisfactory adjustment of it. At present its status is very indefinite. The church is by no means at one concerning it. The pulpit too often evades it. Private Christians waver between the results of independent thought and of early education, undecided whether to approve or condemn; while extremists take advantage of this hesitation to lay down the sternest dogmas, and to thunder denunciations at every head that will not bow to their *ipse dixit*. The questions at issue are not to be dismissed with a sneer at fanaticism and over-scrupulousness on the one hand, and with a protest against unwarrantable liberality on the other. The whole subject must be reëxamined with reference to fundamental gospel principles by both parties, in a spirit of Christian moderation, and with the desire of ascertaining not only what is *safe*, but what is *right*.

To prosecute thoroughly such an examination within the limits assigned me, is, of course, impossible. I can only deal with a few of the great principles underlying the case, and urge their application to a single practical question which has arisen in the experience of our own, and it may be, of other Christian associations.

The idea of *development*, which is perhaps the fundamental one of Christianity, has been to a very great extent swallowed up in the idea of *safety*. It is not an uncommon error to regard Christianity almost exclusively in a defensive aspect; the Christian merely as a *safe* man, protected by Divine safe-guards from temptation, rescued by Divine mercy from the terrors of death and judgment. Correspondingly with this mistake, the tendency has grown to strengthen the defenses of character, rather than to foster its growth. To keep it from temptation, rather than to teach it to overcome temptation. To teach it its danger from the world, rather than its duty to the world. Consequently we have heard more about keeping unspotted from the world, than of going into *all* the world, and preaching the gospel to every creature. More about coming out and being separate, than of knowing the truth which shall make free. More of separating wheat from tares, than of leavening lumps.

The false instinct of self-preservation, which sent the Romanist into cloisters and convents, and tore him from the sweet sanctities of domestic life, has perpetuated itself more than some of us think in Protestant thought and church legislation. And in nothing has this tendency revealed itself more distinctly than in the matter of amusements. For amusement, having the effect to make men feel kindly toward the world, and, more readily than duty, falling in with human inclination, has been regarded as unsafe, and therefore as a thing to be kept at arm's length by the church, and admitted to her folds only under the strictest surveillance, and in gyves and handcuffs.

The developments of this spirit are so familiar that I need not stop to enumerate them. The important thing now is to discover the right stand-point for discussion. And here let me say what, until recently, I had supposed there was no need of saying: that amusement is a necessity of man's nature as truly as food, or drink, or sleep. Physiology, common sense, experience, philosophy, are all at one on this point. Man needs something besides change of employment. He needs something pursued with a view solely to *enjoyment.* Those who deny this are ignorant of the simplest fundamental laws of mind and matter. Men who assert publicly that they need no amusements, and "want to die in the harness," will have the opportunity of dying in the harness some years earlier than would be demanded in the ordinary course of nature. Nature will not suffer even zealous Christian men to violate this law with impunity. She forbids man to labor continuously, and if he persists in disregarding her prohibition, she will revenge herself by imbecility, uselessness, or death.

This must be assumed in all discussions of the subject; and it being a religious, no less than a physical truth, it throws into new prominence the question, how, as Christians, we are to discharge this duty without being led away by the temptation which adjoins it so closely.

Let it be borne in mind that we are not now dealing with individual cases of conscience, but with general laws. While then there is obviously a distinction between amusements—while it is granted that some develop greater capabilities of abuse than others, the attempt to adjust this question on the basis of *discriminating between amusements* must result in failure. It always has, and it always will. This basis is secure only in a question between an innocent amusement, and one involving a palpable violation of the law of God. The advocate of any particular amusement is, on this ground, shut up to the necessity of proving that what he approves and practices is *absolutely pure, and incapable of perversion.* The moment it is admitted that it can, by any possibility, be turned to base uses, the lists are thrown open to all comers, and the utterly insoluble question arises, *just what degree of capacity for perversion entitles an amusement to approval or rejection?* Insoluble, I say, because, not to speak of any other difficulty, one is obliged to confront the fact that no one amusement presents a similar temptation to abuse to all alike. That in which the slightest indulgence might tend to lead one man to ruinous excess, excites no interest in another. It might possibly be dangerous for one man to play at backgammon, while to another it would prove no amusement, but only a tedious method of killing time. On this ground, in short, it is utterly impossible to adjust this matter satisfactorily or consistently. The only consistent or safe rule in this view of the case, is *rigorously to exclude all,* because all are partakers of the universal taint of sin.

"The trail of the serpent is over them all."

It is innocent for boys to play marbles, but sinful to play dominoes. Wherein, pray? They can learn to gamble with one as well as with the other. It is sinful to play billiards, but highly graceful and innocent to play croquet. But why? Really, when it comes to a comparison, the first is infinitely the more beautiful and intellectual game. The ethical distinctions are positively bewildering between balls of ivory and balls of wood; between mallets and cues; between green baize and green grass. A Christian household must not sit down and play at whist, but they are engaged in a Christian and laudable manner if they spend an evening over Dr. Busby, or Master Rodbury cards. Really, it is hard to draw the moral line between cards bearing aces and spades, and cards with the likenesses of Dr. Busby's son and servant, Doll the dairymaid, and the like. When it comes to a question of profit, one is an amusement involving a good deal of healthy, mental exertion, while the other is about as silly and profitless a way of spending an evening as can well be imagined. Youth must not dance, but they may march to music in company, and go through calisthenic exercises, involving a good deal more motion than dancing. But if people may march to music and be guiltless, it is very hard to see how skipping to music converts the exercise into sin. It is said that the *associations* make the difference; but the advocate of this theory is shut up to proving that the associations are inseparable from the amusements. And here is the place to remark that the best amusements are the ones most likely to be abused—the ones which experience shows *are* most abused, and about which cluster the most evil associations. The children of this world are wiser in their generation than the children of light. Men do not care to counterfeit a coin of inferior value; and the world is very clear-sighted to discern the best and richest sources of worldly pleasure, and utterly unscrupulous in appropriating them entirely to itself. The amusements which are most abused, are commonly those which, from their intrinsic value, call most loudly upon virtue to rescue them from their abuses.

The above method of reasoning, in short, will not stand the test of plain common sense. It is trifling, ignoring all distinctions which rest on principles, and substituting factitious ones; and Christians who assume this ground, lay themselves open without defense to the logic and ridicule of any intelligent man of the world who may be disposed to test the reasons for their scrupulousness. They condemn themselves in those things which they allow. The amusements they approve cannot, in many cases, be compared with those which they deprecate, either in elegance, profit, or the amount of intelligence they require.

What point then shall we take for the consideration of this subject? We are confined to one — the stand-point of the Bible. As Christian associations we have but one question to ask: "*What saith the Word.*"

In the New Testament we find little said about the *degrees* of sin. The thought which it throughout tries to impress is, that sin is everywhere; and under any form, or in any degree, is a horrible and fatal thing. The tares are gathered *in bundles* and burned; no matter if one grows a little shorter, and another a little longer. The lustful glance is placed in the same category with the licentious act. The angry thought is of the same piece with the act of murder. The gospel contemplates the sins of the race very much as a man looks at an orange: the rind is full of little protuberances, and a close scrutiny will show that some of these rise higher than others. But nobody pretends to notice these variations; they all spring from one spherical surface, and their variation is not such as to destroy the general effect of roundness. So all these fearful developments of sin spring from one plane, and God hath concluded the whole sinful world in unbelief.

The gospel, therefore, wastes no time in making distinctions between sins, but aims straight at remedying the great fact of *sin* as it exists everywhere. Nor does it leave us in doubt as to its method. It assumes its own power to purify anything, and therefore lays down as its great law of operation, *the law of contact.*

This law it sets forth under a parable: The kingdom of heaven is like leaven, which a woman took and hid in three measures of meal till the whole was leavened. The great truth here illustrated, is the innate power of the gospel to pervade and assimilate to its own nature the whole worldly order of things, just as leaven thus pervades and assimilates the lifeless lumps of dough. This then, is its simple lesson: Put the gospel into contact with everything sinful — the heart of man, the life of man, the employments of man, the amusements of man — into society, its customs, laws, institutions, and it will purge them of evil, and bring them into harmony with the Divine order.

But be sure and note, that the entire success of this action depends upon the contact — upon *the putting the leaven into the lump.* Fail in this, and the lump remains heavy. It matters very little whether the salt have lost his savor or not, if the meat remain in one dish and the salt in the other.

How thoroughly and beautifully this truth was carried out in the life and teachings of Christ, will appear to us more clearly, if we shall recognize the uniform policy of the gospel *to work for the destruction of evil, chiefly through the lodgment and development of good.* Both Christ and his apostles are exhibited in the gospel story as engaged chiefly in asserting and illustrating the truth, and not in combating error. Christ comes into a world lying in wickedness — besotted by it, plagued and tormented by it; full of abominations starting boldly out without pretense of concealment, from every phase of private, social and civil life. But he does not approach these as a mechanic would an old building, saying, "this beam is rotten and must come down; this roof is decayed and must be stripped off; this floor is unsafe and must be pulled up." He does not propose to his disciples to enter upon a wholesale denunciation of profanity and licentiousness. He points out and condemns many of these things it is true; but the main lever of his teaching is the assertion of the great gospel principles. For these he seeks a place of lodgment everywhere. The old tables of the law contained but one commandment that was not prohibitory. Every line portrayed a crime, with a law standing on guard beside it, and warning men away with its "Thou shalt not!" Christ asserts the authority of the law; but in the new table it is seen beckoning toward the commandment, "Thou shalt love the Lord thy God with all thy heart." His instructions to his disciples do not so much concern the things which they are to avoid, as they tend to fix upon their minds right conceptions of his character and mission. So, I repeat, Christ's work is less a crusade against evil, than an assertion of good by precept and example as the surest means in the end of removing evil. Look, too, at Paul at Athens, surrounded by heathen temples, statues and altars. He does not proceed to demonstrate to the curious multitude that the philosophies of Zeno or Epicurus are wrong; or that the worship of Hermes or Athene is absurd.

He throws out at once, bold and stern as a mountain headland, the assertion of the Divine unity, and follows it up with the doctrines of salvation through Christ, the resurrection, and the final judgment. In a few bold strokes he delineates to the astonished skeptics some salient points of natural and revealed religion, and then leaves the truth to germinate and crowd out the evil in its own way and time.

There is indeed a sublimity in this invincible faith in the power of truth exhibited by the Son of Man. In the calmness with which he moves amid the moral ruin that encompasses him, without that anxious haste, and longing for immediate results, which characterize so many modern reformers. The world would have expected a direct and tremendous onslaught upon evil. It would have said that the dropping of a seed of positive truth here and there, would never result in anything. Christ knew better. He knew the latent power of truth; its inherent capability of growth; and he knew that wherever it should find a lodgment, it would grow; and wherever it should grow, it would shake down from its branches, like the mighty tree of the tropics, the germs of a thousand growths like itself. Now it is this very faith in the power of gospel truth, as the most effective destroyer of evil, prompting to put the good boldly into the evil to leaven it, which is sorely needed in the moral movements of the age. Bring the subject of amusements to this test. Compare the action of the church upon it, with the principles so evidently regulating Christ's dealing with evil, and see whether it gains by the comparison. Is it not true, rather, that the Christian world has, to a very large extent, acted upon an entirely opposite principle? It has spent much time in peering into amusements to see what evil they contained, and has kept digging away at this, instead of putting Divine grace into them, in simple faith in God, and letting *that* at once purge and regulate them. It has been so absorbed in ferreting out and declaiming against the evil, as to have forgotten measurably that a corresponding duty lay upon it to develop the good. Overlooking, or at least slighting the great philosophical truth, that amusement is as necessary to man as bread, and fixing its gaze upon the fact that it is capable of perversion, it has most signally failed in the *regulation* of popular amusements, and in teaching how to use, without abusing them. It has withdrawn utterly from many most innocent sources of pleasure; crying, "come out from among them;" they are not *safe;*

Christians must have nothing to do with them. And with its withdrawal, the Devil has come in and taken full possession, and their last state is worse than the first. When the church has touched the subject of amusements, it has generally done so, I think, in a censorious spirit. It has selected certain amusements as sinful, and issued decretals and resolutions against them; it has prescribed penalties against church members who should engage in them; leaving the question in its broader relations untouched. It has fenced off this and that corner of the field of recreation, and put up signs: "*all church members are warned against trespassing on these grounds, under penalty of the law,*" instead of trying to teach Christians how to avail themselves, with profit and safety, of any part of the field. We are cut off from Hamlet, and Lear, and Othello and Macbeth. We cannot avail ourselves of the interpretation of these by the best histrionic talent, because the theater has been suffered to fall so completely into the Devil's hands, that a Christian cannot countenance what is good in it, without at the same time countenancing much that is profane, licentious and indecent. But if the intelligence and culture of a community endeavor to apply the principle I have been advocating, and, in the shape of private theatricals, to furnish a refined, beautiful, and instructive dramatic exhibition, the outcry is little less than if they had leased Wallack's or Niblo's, with a first class troupe; and those Christians who witness it, are condemned as inconsistent and backsliders. Just so with dancing. The idea of Christianity having the remotest connection with this amusement has been scouted as absurd. A procrustean law has been enacted—"*Thou shalt not dance.*" And surely, one would think from some exhibitions of this amusement, that Christian leaven *had* been pretty thoroughly withdrawn from it. One cannot much wonder at the disgust excited by those importations from Paris brothels, the round dances, which, with the present style of female attire, really leave modest men at some loss what to do with their eyes. Let us have as much thundering at these as you will. Let us not mince words. Let ridicule, and sarcasm, and denunciation exhaust their armories, for these are abuses; positive evils. But these abuses are not inseparable from the amusement, which, in proper forms, is healthy, graceful, innocent, and highly commendable. Just here an incident occurs to me which so forcibly illustrates this last remark that I must relate it as the involuntary testimony of an enemy. An amiable and most excellent clergyman of this state, happened to be present one evening when some young ladies went through a quadrille. He looked on with great apparent pleasure. The next morning he was rallied by some of his townsmen on having countenanced dancing by his presence; when he roundly denied the charge, and asserted that no dancing had taken place, but only, as he expressed it, "*a most beautiful exercise.*" Now, I ask, in the name of common sense, why not devote a little Christian care to separating from its abuses, and regulating in its conduct an exercise which improves the bearing of our youth, tends to relieve their natural awkwardness in society, and gives them innocent exhilaration? But no! *Thou shalt not dance.* That is Alpha and Omega. Dancing is liable to abuse, and therefore, O most astoundingly consistent logic, leave it to become a prey to all manner of abuses and abominations. So, if a Christian household makes the attempt to leaven this unfortunate lump, and claims that it can, and does introduce graceful and modest dancing into its family gatherings and social reunions, it is too often denounced as an enemy of Christ and a corrupter of the young. For one I am glad that certain Christian families of high standing in the church of all denominations, have at last asserted their right to act out their own convictions in this matter, and have demonstrated that even this much berated amusement may be elevated, refined, and made a source of social pleasure and profit by the infusion of Christian principle.

One more case in point. When our Young Men's Christian Association of Troy furnished their new rooms, they did so on the principle that prayer meetings and religious periodicals, though important in their place, would not, of themselves, suffice to attract young men from without. They had tried the experiment in their forlorn rooms under a machine shop, in an out-of-the-way place, furnished as a miniature chapel, and a very seedy one at that, and the result was that about six months ago the Association was in a fair way to die, and make no sign. Young men would not go to that dismal hole to spend an evening when more attractive places abounded in the city; and I would not if I had been in their place. But the Association got a new lease of life. It engaged large, airy, pleasant rooms, in a central position. It kept its prayer meeting room neatly and appropriately furnished, but it added a large social parlor, its walls adorned with pictures, a fine piano invitingly open, the best current periodicals, secular and religious, upon the tables, and games of checkers, chess, and dominoes distributed about the room. The young men came in crowds. They were thrown at once into contact with the Christian youth of every church in the city; with the city pastors; with committees, specially appointed by the churches to take strangers in charge, with good music, religious literature, and innocent amusement. For one I thanked God with all my heart. I thought the Association had done a great Christian deed. I hailed it as a happy omen that the Christianity of our city was beginning to see that the Devil had tools which *it* might use to advantage, and was going to take them away from him. But so did not think others who turned their backs on the Association, and denounced it as *encouraging gambling.*

This, in short, is the course pursued to a very great extent with this whole subject of amusements: assuming that the gospel has no business with it except to denounce and warn; taking the leaven away from the lump, instead of putting it in. Creating a wide separation between two things, which, of all others in the world need to be brought into contact — religion and pleasure.

And the practical results of this policy are

before us. It may be said that the tendency now is altogether in the direction of excess; that some Christians are becoming much too liberal, and are fast obliterating all old landmarks. All I have to say to this is, that the more true it is, the better for my position. For, granting, for argument's sake, all that is asserted, this fact shows that there is a reaction from an old and false sentiment, which even if excessive, is a healthy indication. And the one error goes to prove the other; for excessive reactions are pretty sure to grow out of excessive stringency in another direction. At any rate, the great error of the church on this subject is clearly exposed, namely: her failure to regulate amusements. She ought to have been the gospel's instrument in purifying them from abuse; but she has not been. She has been afraid of them; has stood aloof from them; has been almost totally absorbed in detecting their evil tendencies; and, on account of these, forbidding Christians all contact with them. And to-day she stands comparatively powerless in this matter. Church assemblies meet and pass strong and elaborate resolutions on this or that amusement, condemning it, and those who engage in it; and a few persons are deterred by these. But every year the class is increasing that utterly disregards these mandates. It has been said, I know, that in proportion as the church or individuals are engaged in religious efforts, the desire for amusement declines, the implication being that a desire for amusement characterizes only a low state of religion. This deduction is entirely unwarranted, and the process by which it is reached is fallacious.

It is true that in a season of deep religious interest in a church, there will be less disposition to amusements. But the same is true of other than religious interests. Under *any* absorbing, popular excitement, men do not turn to amusement. A special religious interest will draw men's minds from *business* as well as from pleasure; and the inference to the condemnation of business is just as legitimate as to that of amusement.

Again, the statement is not borne out in the ordinary religious life of individuals. Many, very many of the best, most efficient, and most steadily growing Christians in the church exhibit habitually a keen relish for amusements, and for some which are most sternly condemned, and participate in them most heartily.

And once more: while at revival seasons in individual churches, a temporary decrease of amusements may be seen, the more important fact is that the aggregate of Christian society has been for many years past developing a steadily increasing interest in the subject, and a corresponding liberality of sentiment respecting it. Scores of Christian men have billiard tables in their houses. Colleges, from which in years past, students would have been summarily expelled for rolling ten pins, have now bowling alleys of their own. Even in the corridors of staid old Williams the sound of the balls may be heard; and the revival record of the college does not indicate that even this stupendous innovation has wrought to the banishment of the Spirit of God. The assertors of this inverse ratio between piety and amusement must, in short, dispose as best they can, of the fact that along with the growth of Christian intelligence, Christian benevolence, and Christian activity, there has been developed in the church itself a growing sympathy with many of the very forms of amusement most condemned by the religious sentiment of an earlier age.

And this too, not on the part of the careless, and pleasure loving, and half-hearted members of churches, but of men and women high in position in the church; persons of liberal culture and unquestionable piety. These persons, as well qualified to understand the teachings of God's word on this subject as any of the clergy, are asserting their right to act out their own conscientious convictions in their amusements: claiming that they owe to the resolutions of synods, and conventions and conferences, no more than candid and respectful consideration, maintaining the privilege of adopting or rejecting them at pleasure; and accordingly they are throwing open their homes to certain banned amusements, very much to the enhancement of home attractions; very much to the detriment of the saloons; very much to the increase of their children's attachment to home. Church legislation on this subject has been a humiliating failure. It has not compassed its intent. Nay, more, it has overreached itself. It has kept noble and intelligent youth out of the church by insisting on their relinquishment of certain amusements, in the proper and moderate use of which they were unable to see evil. It has tended by this insistence to foster that too common sentiment which paints religion with sombre hues, and couples it with the most forbidding associations. It has tended to drive some to seek in the more liberal atmosphere of Unitarianism the liberty of conscience denied them by orthodoxy; and all this it might have avoided by a clearer recognition of the gospel teaching on this subject: by being less afraid for the purity of the truth, and by throwing Christian presence, and Christian participation, and Christian sentiment boldly into the midst of the people's amusements, with a view less to exscind than to regulate.

I say, "less afraid for the purity of the truth." For Christians shrink from an experiment so bold, especially after so large a proportion of amusements has been usurped by the Devil through their neglect to interfere. The church is shy of a faith in the power of good which comes eating and drinking; which sits at the table of publicans and sinners. The conviction grows on me that Christians have too little faith in the gospel. They do not trust it enough in popular reforms. They realize that evil is a tremendous power, alike to be feared, whether it wear the armor of Goliath, or sing its sweet seductions in the form of a siren; and their instinct of preservation extends beyond themselves to the truth itself. They regard truth as a tender stripling, to be rolled up in mufflers, and suffered to walk out only in charge of certain staid nurses of theory; and not as a man of war in panoply, and with strength enough to take care not only of itself, but of them and their trusted theories too. They are afraid the evil will overwhelm or corrupt the truth; that the leaven, instead of imparting virtue, will be spoiled by the deadness of the lump. We need have no such fear for it. All the developments of the age show that the world needs it in closer contact with its evil than it has ever been yet. It is sometimes urged that in pursuing this course, Christians will bring upon themselves from the world the charge of inconsistency, and moreover will grieve weak Christian brethren. But surely this principle may be pushed too far. With the very fullest recognition of the obligation upon Christians not to let their good be evil spoken of, and not to wrong the weak conscience—concessions made for the sake of Christian charity are surely not required to extend to all the vagaries of individual prejudice, nor to the abandonment of principle. And there is a principle involved in this question of amusements, a principle of far greater importance than many are willing to admit; and to which, if the Christian thought of this age do not take more pains to define it and act upon it, the eyes of the church will be most painfully opened by and by. There is a question here involving not only the enjoyments, but to a great extent the moral welfare of our youth. The young will have amusements, and the question is whether the devil or the church shall furnish them. Whether home, or the ball room, and drinking saloon, and gambling house shall be the more attractive. Whether Christians will resolutely take up good and noble amusements, and give them to youth purged of their evil,— or whether they shall let them remain girt with all their allurements, yet more widely separated from good, and gathering yearly to themselves new elements and associations of evil. Very probably the world, and much of the church will assail the Christian who, in this view of the subject oversteps the line of received opinion, with a cry of inconsistency. But remember that the world judges the church out of its own mouth, independently of the real merits of the case; and requires that it be consistent, not with *their* views, but with its own as publicly expressed. Yet sometimes it is better to be *right* than even to be *consistent;* and if the church has with all sincerity, yet with mistaken zeal, fostered a false sentiment on any subject, do not Christians who discern the error owe to society the benefit of their clearer light? Have they a right to withhold it for fear society should turn on them and call them inconsistent? One would think from a sentiment like this that the gospel process was to be reversed. That not the Christian is to leaven the world, but the world the Christian. Christian sentiment is not to wait for popular sentiment. It claims to be in advance of it. It is to Christians and not to the world that the promise is given, "*Ye shall know the truth;*" and Christian thought, so far from waiting for the movement of these ever shifting popular tides, is the luminary which God has set high in the darkness of this world's sin to draw the tides in his appointed channels. The practical value of truth like that of money, consists in its circulation. It is worth nothing hoarded up or used secretly. If it is ever to be worth anything in correcting false impressions which society may have formed of Christian teaching, it will be by letting it out into society to speak for itself. Nor am I begging the question at issue here. Even an error is better outspoken than cherished in secret. It comes into the field of discussion, and is turned over and examined and exposed, and so truth is the gainer after all. But I think it will be difficult to prove an error in this case. The gospel truth is "*put the leaven into the lump;*" and why the gospel should not be put into our amusements, even into those which are confessedly abused, I cannot see. The more liable to abuse they are, the more they need regulating; and the practical workings of this principle when men have the courage to face prejudice and carry it out, triumphantly vindicate it. The man who furnishes his son a billiard table in his own house, where he can practice that beautiful game with his friends without the adjuncts of liquor and rowdyism, does a good deed. He keeps the youth at home, he keeps his associations under his own eye; he gives him a good, healthy, intellectual amusement purged of its abuses. The college board that erects a bowling alley for the students; that says to young men, "rolling ten pins is not evil, but rolling ten pins in bar rooms, surrounded by drunkards and swearers and indecent pictures *is* evil, and we therefore give you the amusement without these associations, and bid you enjoy it, and draw health and strength from it," — that college board I say, has promoted something more than *muscular* Christianity. It has given the young men a better opinion of religion; has withdrawn them from the influence of temptations to which they expose themselves only because they cannot find the amusements freed from these vile associations. It has drawn just so much patronage from the grog shop. The parents in whose family circle dancing in proper modes and with approved associates and within reasonable hours is encouraged, are doing just so much to keep their daughters from the unhealthy hours,, the immodest displays, and the indiscriminate associations of the ball room. They deserve the thanks, not the reprobation of the church. They are the friends, not the enemies of religion. Let us not be scared by names. Let us not deal, as the pulpit has dealt too much, in vague generalities on this subject. Let us see what those terrible words "billiards" and "dancing," and others of a similar cast mean. Let us see if they are evil and evil only. Let us not assume that our youth are attracted to them only by their native depravity; but see if there be not some goodness, some beauty, some intellectual stimulus which renders them so fascinating. If they need regulating, surely Christian wisdom can regulate them if anything. If any can use them safely, it is Christians who are taught by Divine grace to use this world as not abusing it, and not those who are swayed by impulse and love of pleasure only. But the church does not regulate them, and she never will or can regulate them on the old theory of separation. Never, so long as she persists in wholesale denunciations which she can sustain neither by scripture nor by logic, and against which the common sense of the educated and thoughtful rebels. A more liberal policy in the past, a juster appreciation of the gospel teachings on this subject, would not only have done much towards separating amusements from their abuses, but would have saved her from her present humiliating attitude as the declared enemy of many forms of amusement, from participation in which she has no power to restrain her members.

This principle has been assailed on the ground that the world will abuse it. That they will read in words like these the church's endorsement and license for unlimited indulgence. But if the world draws unwarranted inferences to suit its own depraved wishes, surely that is no reason for suppressing the truth, but rather calls for the full and most careful statement of it. If the world read the gospel wrongly, and wrest it to its own destruction, those who set forth gospel principles are not responsible, unless, as has too often been the case with reference to this subject, the trumpet give an uncertain sound. And the world is too ready to pervert this truth, and does pervert it. Christians, if properly instructed, are so far from being disqualified to use amusements safely, the best qualified of all others to develop their highest uses, and to enjoy without abusing them. The world regards only the permission to enjoy, and ignores the corresponding rule of restraint. In this respect it is like the prince in the Arabian tale, who mounted the enchanted horse, and set him in motion without having informed himself as to the means of guiding or stopping him.

For, let me be clearly understood, I do not lay down this general principle without recognizing the existence of practical limitations to its action, though I assert that the fixing of these limitations belongs chiefly if not entirely to the individual Christian conscience. I have said that the tendency of religious teaching with reference to this and kindred subjects has been to make the idea of *safety* more prominent than that of *development.* Yet I do not overlook, as was implied in the remarks of one who objected to my views, the defensive aspect of the gospel. I admit both the fact and its urgent necessity I could not do otherwise, knowing that the heart is deceitful, and remembering the prayer which Christ puts into every man's mouth, "Lead us not into temptation." I am pleading for the restraints as well as for the privileges of the gospel in the matter of men's amusements; for more and not less care and watchfulness to be brought to bear upon their future regulation.

But withal, I am not bound to abandon the general gospel principle of purging amusements by a closer contact of religion with them, because in certain cases this regulation becomes a matter of extreme difficulty and delicacy ; because I cannot precisely say *how* the gospel leaven is to be conveyed into certain forms of amusement. Just as consistently might I have refused to denounce slavery as a crime against God and humanity because I could not prescribe an effectual scheme for abolishing it. And that such difficulties do arise in the applications of this principle, I freely admit.

There, for example, is the theatre. I believe this principle applies to that as well as to any other amusement. For myself I wish that I could occasionally see Shakespeare interpreted by the best histrionic talent, with all adjuncts of scenery and costume. To me it would be a rich pleasure and a source of intellectual improvement. But as the theatre is now conducted and sustained, I am clearly of the opinion that no Christian ought to frequent it. He cannot do so without, I think, in the great majority of instances, committing himself to very much that is indecent and coarse. And just how this difficulty is to be surmounted, how scholarly, Christian men who love such entertainments and are qualified to profit by them, are to be furnished with them freed from their abuses, I am not now prepared to say. I think it might be done; but the theatre, as it now is, is no place for a Christian.

This, however does not, as before observed, in the least invalidate the general principle. It is merely a question of means. Nor, as was very roundly asserted, does the principle lead to this conclusion that every Christian man must have his box at theatre or opera. It by no means follows that such a course would produce the desired effect. It would be just about as pertinent to argue that because a sewer in a certain street needed cleansing, and because a proper array of men and buckets and brooms would cleanse it, therefore every man and woman on the streets, grave doctors of divinity, stately Mr. Dombey, Flora McFlimsey and Edmund Sparkler, should each shoulder broomstick or bucket, and plunge pell mell into the reeking filth. This argument proceeds upon the assumption that Christians can purge amusements only by using them in the forms and with the appliances attendant upon the world's abuse of them. This is assuming altogether too much. We must get religion into these things, but there are various ways of doing it. You cannot sow broadcast in all soils.

I do not know whether I ought notice one other line of reply to these remarks; but as it seems to be a favorite one, and moreover was adopted by some who I was surprised to see descending to it, I will add a few words on this.

It may be described as an attempt to invalidate a principle by showing that its application to persons of widely different times and circumstances involves an absurdity and then from the absurdity inferring a sin. I do not pretend to give the exact words used, but they were in this style: "Think of Paul dancing; or Peter playing billiards! Do you think we shall have checker-boards in heaven?" And much more of the same kind.

Now this is not argument. It is sheer nonsense; and most unworthy trifling over a serious subject. The reasoning, if it be worthy the name, is simply this; Certain things appear incongruous with our ideas of the character and work of certain men: therefore these things are sinful. It is the easiest thing in the world to invent situations of this kind. Such men as Paul and Peter are associated in our minds with but one set of ideas;—with one great, glorious, solemn work; and their association with any inferior matter affects us unpleasantly at first. Even when we think of Paul making tents, there is at first view something that clashes in our mind with the speech on Mars Hill, and the healing of the cripple at Lystra. But who thinks of disputing from this the propriety of Paul's own hands ministering to his necessities? After all, if there is no sin in rolling ten pins, I know not why Peter should not have participated in that very excellent and healthful recreation with as much propriety as any of the numerous ministers of the present day who "roll" with so much zest and assiduity at our fashionable watering places. Think of Paul dancing! Well, think of him! Think of Paul wearing a blue swallow-tailed coat with brass buttons! How he would have looked under the shadow of the Acropolis, the winds of the Ægean gently swaying his cerulean skirts, and the eager faces of Stoic and Epicurean reflected in the bright buttons! Think of Peter skating; cutting figures of eight, and performing "outer edge backwards!" Think of John in a white cravat; or of Bartholomew putting up seidlitz powders; or of Timothy running with a fire-engine! How WOULD they have looked? Therefore hasten ye trim gentlemen, to doff your guilty blue and brass, and don the toga. Lay aside your skates, boys. Peter would have looked very strangely skating, therefore it is sinful to skate. Tear off your white chokers, ye Reverends, and throw away your pestles ye apothecaries, and be like the apostles. Shall we have checker-boards in heaven? No, brother, I presume not. Neither shall we marry, nor be given in marriage; but pray don't condemn us to celibacy on that ground while we remain upon earth. "Would you play chess on your death-bed?" Probably not, my friend. Neither would I put on my boots, or do a great many other very innocent things. Death stands out in startling contrast to *all* our employments: to business and study, as well as to recreation; and you would find it vastly inconvenient to act upon the principle that nothing must be done which you would not do on your death-bed.

But enough of this. I come now to the one practical application of these principles out of which this whole discussion has grown.

When our Troy Christian Association adopted the practice of introducing games into their rooms, I gave it my hearty approval. My opinion on this subject has been confirmed by what I have seen and heard of the results of the experiment.

It was based on the principles I have been advocating in this paper, and on the farther consideration, growing out of these, that we must take some of the devil's weapons and sanctify them before we could successfully fight him on his own ground. As remarked already, prayer-meetings will not draw irreligious young men into the sphere where we want them. Give them first well lighted and warmed apartments, handsomely furnished, where they can find music and books and newspapers and games, and you stand some chance then of drawing them into the prayer-meetings. And indeed the direct religious influence of these associations, while highly important, is nevertheless subordinate to their work in bringing young men into contact with the various churches of the community, where the religious appliances are of course more perfect. The great point is to get them into some position where the churches can reach them. They will not come to church, many of them, when they first enter the community. The church has but limited facilities for finding them out in their stores and boarding-houses and schools; and it may find therefore a powerful auxiliary in these associations, which bring the stranger youth where it can bring its influences to bear on them. But for this purpose the place of rendezvous must be made attractive. We must have head-quarters as pleasant as the devil's. I hope all of you have read the article in *Guthrie's Sunday Magazine* for January, 1866, entitled "*The house that beats the public house;*" that splendid iron structure in Colne, Lancashire, built expressly for the irreligious working class. There are fountains, and pictures, and games, cabinets and books and newspapers. There are quiet reading rooms, there are refreshment rooms, even smoking rooms. There is a school room, there are musical entertainments on stated nights, there are religious services on Sabbath evenings. "On Christmas eve, 1863," says the writer, "the musicians at one of the public houses piped for some time, but no dancers presented themselves, till at length the players themselves adjourned to the meeting at the Iron School. An attempt to open the theatre that winter failed through the same influence. The actors, after struggling for a week in the face of empty benches, left the place in despair."

Here is a clear and successful recognition of the truth that religion has not such strong alliance with the unregenerate heart that she can afford to dispense with all legitimate aids and recommendations. The firemen have their upper parlor in the engine house furnished richly and tastefully. The drinking saloons are invested with all the attractions that marble, and glass, and drapery and pictures can give them. One man who appeared last week before the excise commissioners, said he had expended ten thousand dollars in fitting up his saloon. He knew it would pay; and we cannot expect irreligious young men to be drawn away from these by mere religious appliances. We must employ other attractions. We must make our houses beat the public houses. We must sanctify new forces for this end. Pictures and cabinets, carpets and draperies, music and games are not the devil's any more than they are ours. Young men will have some retreat beside their comfortless boarding-houses; some society besides their landlord's family, and it is a match between the devil and the church which of us shall furnish these. Depend upon it, if the church do not give them amusement, regulated on a liberal Christian basis, the devil will give them abundance that is unregulated. God forbid that Christian squeamishness should suffer them to turn aside to the house whose gates lead to hell, and to habits which shall make mothers curse the day they gave them birth.

I will give two incidents showing the practical working of this new system in the Troy Association. A member of my church, walking in the street one evening, saw three young men just before him, and overheard one say to the others, "Come, let's go and take a drink." One of the others replied, "No, I don't care to take a drink. Let's go to the Christian Association Rooms." "Pshaw!" said the third, "I don't want to go there to prayer meeting." "No, no," was the response; "they've got a right nice place there, and we can have a good time." He went on describing the rooms, and then added: "*and they're for just such fellows as we are.*" He gained his point, and they followed him to the rooms.

Three clubs of young men, or boys rather, were broken up soon after the new rooms were opened. I do not know their character fully, but have been told that drinking was practiced at their meetings. They now frequent the rooms of the society, and pay over into its treasury their club subscriptions. There are many more of such cases. They speak with trumpet tongues as to the value of this policy. They show that its practical influence is against the groggery and the gambling saloon, and if it work no other result, that of itself is vindication enough.

And now I leave the subject. I do not shrink from the application of this Bible principle to our amusements. The other, the separative policy, the keeping of leaven and lump apart, has been tried, and has failed, utterly failed.

Will it not be well to try another policy? I want for our youth a Christianity that shall not relax one iota of its obligation to God or to man. That shall not bate one jot from an entire consecration of heart and life to God; that shall walk closely with God, and feel as deeply as human weakness can feel, the necessity of watchfulness and of divine care to keep it from temptation. I challenge any man to draw undue license from the principles I have asserted. But I want more joy brought out of the world by Christians. I want the gospel carried boldly into some things from which it has been kept aloof. I want Christian life to be in the spirit more than in the letter. I do not plead for less but for more conformity to the spirit and teaching of Christ. Not for a lower but for a higher Christian life; for a wider application of gospel principles, a more implicit trust in the leavening power of truth; a more practical belief in the assertion that the weapons of our warfare are mighty through God to the pulling down of strongholds. I want Christian conscience clothed with principles and not with dogmas. I want the word of God read and interpreted fairly, and that allowed which it allows. I protest against its being twisted and perverted into rules for the unnecessary abridgment of Christian liberty, where it lays down only general principles for the conscience. I want less of the religion that is

> "Dark as a funeral scarf from stem to stern,"

and more of that which is full of child-like trust in the love of God and the power of truth, and of freedom purged by love from license.

THE TRUE NONCONFORMIST.

A

COMMUNION SERMON

DELIVERED SEPT. 16, 1866,

IN THE

FIRST PRESBYTERIAN CHURCH, TROY, N. Y.

THE TRUE NONCONFORMIST.

ROM. xii, 2. "*And be not conformed to this world: but be ye transformed by the renewing of your mind, that ye may prove what is that good, and acceptable, and perfect will of God.*"

By itself, this command is ambiguous. Common sense testifies that, in very many things, every Christian *must*, more or less, conform to the world. Many of the world's customs are not only harmless, but salutary, beautiful, ennobling, necessary to the very being of society. We need some test by which to interpret this command.

Let us first endeavor, as a means of discovering it, to clear away a preliminary error, viz.: the not uncommon idea that difference from the world is a matter of any value or consequence of itself. A great many persons, lamenting over real or supposed deficiencies of Christians, make this the staple of their complaint; *you cannot distinguish them from the world:* and when urging upon them some duty, or the relinquishment of some practice, enforce it by the argument,

Christians should aim to be distinct from the world.

There is truth in this, but there is also falsehood. Christians, *real* Christians, will always be distinct from the world, and the distinction will be very clearly defined. But Christians should not make it their *object* to be distinct from the world. They should aim to be Christians, and let the distinction follow in its natural order and degree. Singularity, in itself, is no virtue. It is just as likely to be a vice. A man is not necessarily better because he is unlike the rest of the world. Difference from the world, therefore, is not an *end* of Christian discipline, but a result and concomitant of it. This distinction is of the utmost importance. If distinctiveness is regarded as an *object* of Christian effort, its value is sacrificed. Its tendency is to formality; to the substitution of a variety of *outward* standards of duty for a single *inward* regulative principle. To pride and self-righteousness on the ground of singularity. Such have been its developments, for instance, in certain religious sects who insisted on plainness of dress as a duty. Undoubtedly the spirit which originally prompted the requisition was good, Christlike. It was the desire to take from the useless adornment of the person and bestow upon objects of Christian effort and charity. It was the desire to remove temptations to vanity and idle display. But in too many cases these things were forgotten. Christians received the precept in the letter and not in the spirit. They came to insist on plainness of dress as a mark of a true Christian, and forgot that materials of plain or sad colors might be as costly and rich as gayer ones. They came to pride themselves on their plainness as a distinction from the rest of the world. They said bitter and unchristian things against the man who should carry a gold watch or the woman who should wear a feather or a ribbon. They perverted scripture to uphold this ridiculous whim, and brought scorn upon themselves and reproach upon the cause of Christ, because they turned their eyes from the inward, regulative power of the gospel to one of its natural developments, and looked at that until it grew out of all proportion.

How then are we rightly to apply this command?

The apostle, in giving us an answer, takes up the question at the very point at which most inquirers do, viz.: at the matter of *sacrifice.* For this is the way in which it presents itself to most minds. In order not to be conformed to the world, I must sacrifice much that is of the world. What, now, may I retain, and what must I relinquish?

And in Paul's answer, he strikes directly at any such method of putting the question. Nonconformity to the world involves sacrifice, it is true, but not a sacrifice made in any such spirit as this — a spirit that ere it gives itself to Christ, sits down and begins to sort its possessions, pleasures, pursuits, into two piles, saying: "this for God, this for the world: this goes back to my treasure house, this I throw away." Not so. He sweeps the whole into one heap, and says, "I beseech you brethren, by the mercies of God, that ye *present your bodies a living sacrifice, and be transformed by the renewing of your mind.*" He asks that the *whole man*, with all his belongings, be made an offering to God, even as he says in another place, "the very God of peace sanctify you *wholly*, and I pray God your whole spirit and soul and body be preserved blameless unto the coming of our Lord Jesus Christ. He rises above details of sacrifice to a sacrifice which includes and regulates all details; and in so doing he is but insisting upon the precept of Christ: "If any man will be my disciple, let him *deny himself.*' 'And notice particularly the meaning of this precept which is so generally but half understood. It is not, let him cut himself off from this thing or that thing, but let him *deny himself;* literally, let him *say that self is not*, and that the will of Christ is *everything*. Holding fast this principle a man cannot greatly err. The will of Christ and the will of the world are so diametrically opposite, that he cannot go toward the one without going away from the other. A man has no business to waste time pondering over the *details* of his sacrifice for Christ's sake, tormenting himself with deciding between what is right and what is wrong; what is worldly and what is heavenly. The will of Christ once heartily embraced as a rule of life will teach him to decide. Christ received into the heart will regulate its affinities and repulsions. The law of the *spirit* of life in Christ Jesus shall make the soul free from the law of sin and death, so that it shall hate the things it once loved, and love those it once despised.

Young people often come to their pastor saying: "If I become a Christian, must I give up such and such things? Must I discharge such and such duties?" And for myself I reply to them—"I have no answer to give you. I will not encourage you to come to Christ in this mean, bargain-making spirit. If your conscience tells you a thing is wrong, as it does in many cases, you have no need to ask me if Christ will require its relinquishment. You know he will, without any compromise. But when it comes to any doubtful matter, waive that question. You have nothing whatever to do with it now. Christ requires of you to be willing to obey him implicitly in all things, without regard to your own feelings or preferences, your own prosperity or safety, no matter what duties or sacrifices obedience involves; and I simpy ask you *are you willing to do this?* If you are not, Christ does not want you. A young man goes to a recruiting office to enlist. The sergeant examines him, and says: "you are just the kind of man I want. Here, put down your name. Your bounty is so much; your pay will be so much." The recruit takes the pen in his hand, but stops suddenly in the act of writing his name, and says: "How far shall I be required to march daily? What kind of a tent shall I have? Must I do picket duty beyond regular hours? To what kind of a climate am I to be sent?" How long do you suppose the officer would keep patience with such a man? How many of these questions would he pretend to answer, even if he could? He would simply say to the man: "we make no terms with you, sir, beyond your bounty and pay. If you enlist, you do so with the understanding that a soldier has nothing to do but obey orders; to serve where, when, and how he may be directed. If you want to know these things, enlist, and you will find out when you are in service. Just so I say to one who begins inquiring into the details of Christ's service: If you want to find out, enlist. Commit your life to Christ's keeping. Devote yourself to Christ's service, and "if any man *wills* to do his will, he shall know of the doctrine." An inquirer for salvation, tormenting himself about what he must do and what relinquish, forgets that he is in no condition to decide such a question. To decide it he wants just that spiritual insight and those new affinities which faith in Christ and the consequent renewal of his nature will give him. He wants to see these things from a stand-point which he has not yet attained. He had far better let them go for the present, and concentrate his resolution on this one point: "I give myself to Jesus without reserve. Whatever he tells me I may enjoy I will endeavor to enjoy in his love and fear. Whatever he bids me cast away, though it be a right hand, I will cut it off and cast it from me." A young man once came to me saying: "There seems to be but one thing in the way of my entire surrender to Christ. If I become a Christian, and a member of the church, I don't see how I can ever take any public part in the religious meetings. If I could only decide whether God required this of me, I think my way would be clear." I said to him, "My brother, you are not called on to settle that question now. You have no means of deciding it. You had better drop it altogether for the present. God has promised that if you will commit your ways unto him he will direct you. Now I believe you sincerely want to do God's will, and that you are ready, whenever he shall show it you, to pledge yourself to do your duty. Leave the matter there; and if, at any time, this duty should be thrust upon you, do it in God's name and strength." He soon after joined the church, and has borne himself since with a fidelity and devotion which speak well for the thoroughness of the work of grace in him.

Now this is what the apostle means by a *living* sacrifice. This spirit of consecration infused into sacrifice fills it with life. The sacrifice becomes "living" only when self dies; when the man says

"Here Lord, I give myself away:
'Tis all that I can do."

The other method of securing nonconformity to the world by acting for the mere sake of difference or according to circumstances, constitutes a dead sacrifice. Such were the sacrifices of the Pharisees. They thanked God they were not as other men; but the difference was but outward. To the spectator's eye they were not conformed to the world. They did not dress like it. Their prayers were longer and more frequent. They did not eat with publicans and sinners. But these differences had become the chief end of their religious life. Their development was like arranging the limbs of a corpse for exhibition. They were not the natural, spontaneous outgrowths of a living inward principle; and hence the Pharisees have passed into history as the representative hypocrites of all time.

The essential character of this self-sacrifice will farther appear from a correct understanding of the phrase *reasonable service.* On this, two things must be remarked. 1st, that the expression does not belong to the words "*living sacrifice*" alone, but to the whole exhortation. In other words, it is not the *living sacrifice* which is a reasonable service, but the presenting the bodies a living sacrifice, "holy, acceptable unto God." 2dly, it is to be noted that the expression "*rea-*

sonable service" is very commonly misunderstood to mean a service which is proper or becoming; which we have the best of all reasons for rendering. This is all true; but this is not what the text means. It signifies a service whose main spring is in the *thinking*, *reasoning*, *spiritual* department of man's nature—a spiritual service rendered to a God who is a spirit, and who requireth to be worshiped in spirit and in truth. Of such Peter says: "ye also, as lively stones, are built up *a spiritual house*, a holy priesthood, to offer up *spiritual sacrifices* acceptable to God by Jesus Christ." In pursuance of this idea, the apostle, in our text, after speaking of the presenting of *the body* as a living sacrifice, and of such a presentation as a *reasoning* service, gives us the key to the whole thought by his final exhortation, "be ye transformed by the *renewing of your mind;*" so that it is clear that the outward conformity of the body to God's will, is made both a living sacrifice and a reasoning service by having its mainspring in a renewed mind. Only thus will the body be offered alive to God. Only thus will the mind be truly transformed. All the outward developments of the life will then bear the stamp of a reasoning service. The way of peace will be chosen from conviction. The will, self-impelled, will set toward God. The conscience will be alive with a divinely inspired sensitiveness. All the affections and desires, of their own accord, will stretch their hands towards Christ, and the renewed man will daily realize that the water which Jesus gives is *in* him, living water, springing up into everlasting life.

It is then clear, I think, from what has been said, that nonconformity to the world is not the *aim*, but one of the incidents of Christian life. The Christian's *aim* is distinctly stated here to be the proving of the will of God—that which is good, acceptable and perfect. Yet nonconformity to the world will develop itself as a *necessary incident* of Christian living. Being transformed by the renewing of the mind, the outward life will necessarily be transformed also, and will cease to be conformed to the world. The soul which desires that which is good, acceptable, perfect, can no longer find affinity with that which is bad, imperfect, and displeasing to God. The differences are not incidental, they are generic. The Christian and the world belong to different orders; are regulated by different laws. The Christian is, as it were, grafted upon the new stock, and can no more bear the fruit of his old sinful life, than the ingrafted branch can bear its former fruit.

Old things have passed away. All things have become new. He is a new creature in Christ Jesus. These differences have not to be marked by finely drawn lines of casuistry. There are indeed points at which the worldly and the Christian life run for a little way parallel. Points where neither party can very well act differently from the other. But for all that, the divergence is wide enough at many other points to leave no doubt. I am speaking now of *true* Christians, thoroughly renewed in the spirit of their mind; courageous, unflinching, consistent Christians: not of those whifflers and compromisers who call themselves Christians, and who try to trim between God and the world, so as to relinquish no advantages on the side of either. A man cannot live many hours by the rule of Christ without coming into direct issue with the world. And now, as to these points of difference. They are, of course, too numerous to be dealt with in detail, and I can, therefore, only call your attention to one or two classes of them.

1st. On which I need not dwell, is the class of *worldly sins.* Of course the transformed man will not be conformed to the world in these. Not that a Christian never errs, by any means, but that the general current of his life will set in the direction of pleasing God, and away from those things which are plainly contrary to his will.

2d. A marked difference develops itself in the region of the motives, the tempers, the dispositions, and the principles of action. Sometimes it is difficult to pronounce upon these differences with certainty, yet some of them are easily recognizable. Two men will often do precisely the same thing from different motives. A Christian and a worldly man, for example, are foully abused by a profane ruffian. Both receive the abuse in silence, and go their way without bestowing any attention upon him. But the two are commonly actuated by very different impulses. The one turns away with anger and loathing, and is silent because it is beneath his dignity to reply, or to notice the aggressor. The other, though tempted to anger, remembers the example of him whom he serves. Who, when he was reviled, reviled not again: and leaves the railer, striving to pity his ignorance, and to forget his insult. Pride accomplishes, outwardly, in the one case, what Christian humility does in the other. So in cases of great affliction. It is sometimes hard to decide, from outward indications, whether divine grace or native force of will is the stronger. The worldly man will exhibit equal composure with the Christian; will seem for the time to accept the visitation with no less equanimity than the other. But those who are much with men under such circumstances, and come perhaps as close to their hearts as it is possible for man to do, recognize a very decided difference. They know that the composure which springs from stoicism, iron nerve, indomitable will, is a different thing from that which is born of submission and resignation to the will of God. That the one but crowds the sharp grief deeper into the heart, and shuts up the fountain of healing tears, and makes the man hard and sullen and defiant, and chills his sympathies, and disposes him to solitary brooding, and after all, gives way at last, and leaves him a broken reed, while the other finds in the breach which God made in his cherished plans, an opening through which heaven smiles on him, rises on the ruins of his wrecked hopes to a purer and more unselfish life, draws sweetness out of his sorrow, and wins a firmer trust in God, and a deeper and more comprehensive sympathy for his sorrowing brethren everywhere. These differences are endless. They cover every variety of experience. The world talks of the dignity of man, asserts his knowledge and his unimpaired judgment. The Christian distrusts his deceitful heart and fallen nature, and becomes a little child that he may know the truth. The world walks by sight and sneers at faith. Faith is the Christian's atmosphere, out of which he cannot breathe freely. The world talks of law, the Christian of providence. The world knows God, either vaguely, as a deity to be feared for his power, and but dimly apprehended by man, or as a mere aggregate of laws divorced from any real, apprehensible personality. The Christian communes and walks with him daily as a tender, loving, and wise father.

But I hasten to a third class of differences, with which I shall deal more at length: I mean those which appear in the Christian's conduct respecting those things which he uses in common with the world. Under this head falls that large class of actions, which, *in themselves considered*, have no moral value, but acquire one from the end they are made to serve, the manner in which they are pursued, or the motive in which they originate. On these arise the most perplexing of all moral questions, the most subtle cases of conscience, and too often, I grieve to say, the most acrimonious discussions. Under this head are included most of those vexed questions as to amusements, dress, meat and drink, and the like. And this text,

I am sorry to say, has been made the basis for inculcating some most false and pernicious doctrines concerning these things.

Now it seems to me that very many of the difficulties which arise on these subjects are quite unnecessary, and would be in great part destroyed by resting upon the simple, unequivocal testimony of the Bible. I do not think that God's Word is at all wanting in explicitness on these points. Here is this text for instance. Nothing can be plainer. It tells us our first great duty is to submit our wills to God's will; to commit ourselves to his guidance without reserve, a living sacrifice; to be transformed; and that when this shall have been done, we shall know what the will of God is; we shall practically prove what is good and acceptable and perfect, and, as a matter of course, shall not be conformed to the sinful principles and practices of the world. Now it follows from this that whatever is good and acceptable and perfect, not opposed to the new principle of life in us, is ours, given us by God to use and enjoy; and that in the use and enjoyment of it within the limits he prescribes, we *are not conformed to the world* in any bad sense. I say this, well aware that every one of these things contains capabilities for abuse, and that the world does most sadly abuse them; and this brings me directly to my point that the difference between Christians and the world as respects these things is to be developed *in the proper use and regulation by Christians of what the world abuses.* Christians are not to be driven from every point which the world sees fit to occupy by the hue and cry of nonconformity. They are to remember that in these things there is a duty to be done as well as a pleasure to be enjoyed, and that they are to show their nonconformity, not by abandoning, but by refusing to conform to the world's excesses, and by insisting on the restraining principles of God's Word. Let us here hold closely by the opening thought of our discussion, that conformity to the world *in itself* is no sin, and nonconformity *in itself* no virtue. Conformity to the world is sinful when the world's practice is sinful and not otherwise.

Now this is a very plain rule. It is Christ's rule. Paul takes it directly from Christ. But I am aware that another question enters here, namely, that of expediency. There may be private considerations tending to make the relinquishment of a harmless thing expedient for you or for me. There may be considerations growing out of your relations to others which may render use inexpedient. In such cases, expediency, of course, assumes *to you* the obligation of law. But as regards these cases no man can decide for you. The Bible throws them on your own conscience. Let every man be fully persuaded *in his own mind.* Expediency is a matter for individuals. No law can be laid down for it. The two things necessarily exclude each other. If you lay it down that such a course is expedient for *every one,* you remove the matter at once from the region of expediency, and put it on the ground of law; and this course no man nor body of men is ever justified in pursuing. Such a step trenches on the sacred enclosure of the individual moral sense, a holy of holies, into which man and his Maker alone enter. At the same time, abundant light will be given to every humble, faithful child of Christ, to settle these questions of expediency. When love to God is the moving principle of a man's life, it develops in him an insight which guides him unerringly through questions where casuistry would become hopelessly entangled. You may see the same truth illustrated in your own homes. See that loving, obedient child, whose highest delight is to perform your behest and anticipate your wishes. How very few errors that child commits, even in cases where you have laid down no rule. It reaches the knowledge of your wishes through a kind of instinct as reliable as it is undefinable. Surely faith ought to teach us to expect a clew through such mazes from a Father who has promised that he will direct the paths of those who acknowledge him.

And here, I insist, whether the question be one of law or of expediency, has been a grave error of the church in not trusting enough to this inward principle of life in the soul, to this insight of love, to regulate the outward developments of the life, and to prevent the obliteration of the lines between the church and the world. She has busied herself too much with details, and not enough with that which lies back of them; too much with the circumference and not enough with the centre. Christ teaches us that if the fountain be pure, the streams must be pure. But the church, in her unconscious distrust of the purifying power of the fountain, has thrown into the streams such abundance of mint, anise, and cummin, that the taste of the original water is sometimes sadly impaired. Too often, while she has been busy with the streams, the fountain head has been gathering unsuspected poison. While I recognize the church's duty to watch carefully over Christ's flock, to counsel, rebuke, restrain, I think that she has encouraged, in many cases, by her want of faith in the power of the relation between Christ and the believer, an artificial religious life, a factitious conscience, a life wanting the freedom and naturalness of movement properly engendered by the gospel. I think she should have insisted more on having this clearly defined and constantly maintained, more on a full assurance, and a lively faith, and an ever burning love, and less on details which these would have regulated of themselves. I believe that if she had done this, and moreover had preached the word literally and boldly to the people, had told the people their privilege to use God's gifts, and pointed them to the principle of love to God as competent to regulate use, and not twisted its declarations into warrants for the abridgment of Christian liberty,— there would be in the church to-day more simple, strong, manly, intelligent piety, and far less conformity to the world. This distinction between safe and unsafe truths is a Romish and not a Protestant idea; and the temporary gain secured by acting upon it is more than counterbalanced by the final pernicious result.

It is far safer for me and for you that I preach this truth to you boldly and plainly; and I have a special object in bringing it to your notice now, at this solemn season when you are reviewing the past, and making a new consecration of yourselves to the service of Christ.

Here, as you renew your original vow to come out from the world, it is well that you do this with no vague idea of what you promise. What I shall now say applies to most if not all of you, but especially to the younger members of the church. As you enter upon a season of special religious activity, you also enter upon a season which society is wont to devote largely to pleasure. Ere another communion season shall have come round, the season for evening entertainments and festal gatherings, will be at its height. From the nature of circumstances you will be called upon to participate in these more or less; and it is at these points that the temptation to conformity to the world will be most likely to assail you.

Most of you are probably aware of the ground I have recently taken before the public on the subject of amusements; a position which has excited considerable comment, and some censure. I do not see why it should. There is nothing novel in my views on this subject. I have merely stated the gospel principle, the principle which Christ propounded, and by which he lived — that the proper and only way to preserve our pleasures or anything else from abuse, is to put Christian leaven into them. That our duty in such matters, is not to give them over bodily to the devil and to the world, to be abused and perverted at their pleasure; but to save them from such perversion, and make them legitimate instruments of Christian joy and growth, by using them in the name and under the law of Christ. If these things are evil, we have no right to have anything to do with them. If they are, though not evil in themselves, so under the dominion of evil, and so dependent upon evil for support, as the theatre, for example, is, that Christian participation cannot separate them from their abuses, we ought to abandon them. But as to the general principle, that it is abuse and not proper use which Christ condemns, and that many of the things which the devil has usurped, are as much yours as his, there can be no doubt. I have not one word to modify or retract of what I have written on this subject. Challenged, I would reiterate it word for word, if I knew I should go from this pulpit to my grave. And I dare any Christian to draw from what I have written, or from what I have said to-day, license for improper conformity to the world. If you do so, depend on it, *you* and not *I* will be condemned. And I rejoice especially to-day, in having assumed this position; because I have never had so good ground from which to counsel you as to your intercourse with the world of pleasure. If I were to put this matter to you on the ground of men's rules and decrees, if I were to try and show you, by subtle hair-splitting, that this thing is one degree more capable of abuse than that thing; and that, therefore, you may use that, and must abandon this, I should expose myself to merciless logic, and to just ridicule. I leave this ground entirely. I put myself on God's word, and say to you this morning, be not conformed to this world. I say to you as the first, the indispensable requisite for deciding in what conformity consists, see that your relations to Christ are properly adjusted. Present yourselves living sacrifices to him. Be transformed by the renewing of your mind. Submit your will to the will of God without reserve. Then shall you be able to prove what is his will, what is good and acceptable and perfect. Then shall your judgment be so enlightened as to enable you to render a reasoning, a reasonable, a thoughtful and discriminating service. This is the first thing.

For this I pray for you. For this I am anxious for you, that you be vitally united to Christ; that you have a living, active faith in him; a clear witness of your acceptance with him, an ever burning love for him. If you have these, I know that the details of your lives, whether they concern your pleasures, or your business, or your studies, will take care of themselves. But remember this prerequisite. Do not go away saying, "my pastor says I may lawfully indulge in this or that, and I need give myself no further trouble about it." I say to you no such thing. I say that you want your whole nature renewed by the indwelling of Christ, and that without this you are not safe in the world one moment. That without this you are in continual danger of conformity to the world. Without this you are in no condition to decide in what you may engage, or how far you may engage in it without abuse. Withal, you *will* need to trouble yourself about these matters; to study God's law; to watch closely your own heart and life; to avoid needless temptation; to exercise strong resolution when pleasure beckons you beyond the bounds erected by Christian duty. I bid you rejoice in your youth. I bid you use those amusements which are innocent in themselves, freely and with grati tude to God, but to beware of their abuse. I can safely tell you some things which God's word will teach you as to this matter. It will tell you that where you make pleasure the end and rule of your life, and duty the exception, you are guilty of abuse. It will tell you that when pleasure saps the fountains of your health, when it steals away your hours of sleep, and tempts you to excessive indulgence of appetite at an hour which nature prescribes for the rest and recuperation of your organs, when it leads you to expose yourself to sickness by inadequate clothing—it is a gross abuse for which God will hold you accountable. It will tell you that when any description of pleasure trenches on the limits of modesty, it is an abuse; that the public embracing of young men and women in the vile dances of the day, is an offense against decency, an abomination against which manly nobleness and maidenly delicacy ought to cry out with all their power. It will tell you that when pleasure of any kind interferes with your covenant obligations to the church, and keeps you from the ordinances of God's house, it is an abuse; a conformity to the world, against which God warns you in this text.

Come then and give yourselves to Christ, not

repelled by any false, ascetic views of his religion, but believing, as his word entitles you to believe, that it is the promoter of innocent joy, of healthy and grateful recreation, of the highest and purest pleasures. Come, and he shall show you by his own life how to be in the world, yet not of it. How to live in strictest conformity to duty, and yet be free indeed, and exhibit to the world a broad, noble, generous Christian life — a life in the spirit and not in the letter. He shall teach you to live by the insight of love, and not by the prescriptions of a bare scheme of duty. Oh, that you may grow to the stature of perfect men and women in Christ; that you may be living examples of a reasoning service, models of a piety, enthusiastic yet judicious; all aglow with the love of Christ carried into every detail of your lives, into your pleasures, your conversation, your business; bringing everything, great and small, into conformity with the law of Christ, and making the whole life move sweetly and harmoniously round him. You will not then be a worldly church. You will not then be stumbling blocks to the kingdom of Christ. You will be living epistles, read and known of all men, and they, seeing your good works, shall glorify your father which is in Heaven.

THE
CHURCH AND THE YOUNG MAN.

A SERMON

DELIVERED

ON SABBATH MORNING, NOVEMBER 4, 1866,

IN THE

FIRST PRESBYTERIAN CHURCH, TROY,

AT THE REQUEST OF

THE YOUNG MEN'S CHRISTIAN ASSOCIATION.

THE CHURCH AND THE YOUNG MAN.

2 SAM. xviii, 5. "*And the king commanded Joab and Abishai and Ittai saying, deal gently for my sake with the young man, even with Absalom.*"

There are few passages of Holy writ more beautiful or suggestive than this. Notwithstanding the astounding character of Absalom's rebellion; though the mind of the sovereign and father of his people is torn with indignation at this outrage upon his throne and person, and is busy with plans for the security of his kingdom and the repulse of the invader; though David is stunned and bewildered at this high handed display of ingratitude and rebellion on the part of his favorite child, the father finds place to assert itself amid the cares of the sovereign, and to breathe a word of caution to his generals respecting the person of his dearly loved boy.

In accordance with the request of the Young Men's National Christian Convention to the churches, I propose to devote this service to a discussion of their relations to the church. I take this text as setting forth a similar charge given by our Lord and King Christ to his militant church, to deal gently with the young man. I therefore invite your attention to the following points respecting the relations of young men to the church:

I. The church *must* deal with them.
II. The church *ought* to deal with them.
III. How the church should deal with them.

I. *The church must deal with young men.*

Absalom, however foolish and wicked his revolt, however strange his rebellion against his royal father, notwithstanding his youth and inexperience, was a stubborn fact, with which the leaders and counselors and armies of the kingdom found themselves obliged to deal. Otherwise David would have been dethroned and his authority violently usurped. If not dealt with so as to suppress him, he must be dealt with in the more unpleasant capacity of a suppressor and tyrant.

Young men are a fact in society; and as such cannot be without relations to the church. Not only so, they are an important fact; a prominent fact; a potent fact. They are a force in the business, the social, the political, the governmental relations of the community. If they have not wisdom, they have strength and energy. If they have not caution, they have enterprise. If they have not experience, they have tact, intelligence and knowledge. If they refuse to follow old rules, they succeed ofttimes in the use of their own methods. Society concedes much to them, entrusts them with serious responsibilities, seeks them for positions of power and influence, is powerfully swayed in whatever direction they choose, as a body, to throw themselves, applauds and welcomes their success.

The relations of such a body to the church of Christ must be important. This mass of manly strength, energy, independence, intelligence and enterprise must, if set on fire with Christian ardor and enlisted on her behalf, greatly conduce to her prosperity; while it cannot but be a serious hindrance to her success if this element is neutral, or arrayed against her. If neutral, indeed, it *is* against her. If she have not the young men incorporated with her membership, at work in her sabbath schools, in regular attendance on her ordinances, woven into her social relations, throwing their strength and generosity and enthusiasm into her benevolent enterprises, contributing their fresh thought to her assemblies, working, through the closer intimacies which mark their age, to increase her numbers, she will have to move under the drag applied by their indifference, resist their fascinations exerted in drawing others away from her standard, contend sharply against the skepticism to which youth is naturally prone, and if they are won at last, win them when the freshness of youth is gone, and by a double expenditure of power. The church *must* deal with them as the friends or as the enemies of religion; must appropriate or resist their power. They come to her in the flush of their manly strength, like the Roman envoys to Carthage, holding in their robes peace and war, and offering the church her choice.

II. *The church ought to deal with them.*

1. In simple consistency with her own principles. Not only to touch them where she must, but where she can. Not to regard them as aside from her peculiar work, but as constituting a peculiarly important and interesting part of her work. She professes to labor for the salvation of men, where can she find excuse for failing to provide *special* appliances if need be, for the salva-

tion of young men? She professes to be an *educator* as well as an evangelizer. Here is material in its most inviting shape, and at the stage best adapted for her moulding. She professes to provide for the extension of her doctrine and spirit. Can she, with any show of reason, neglect the force furnished her in this mass of youthful energy and enthusiasm. She professes to rescue men from danger. Does she see any danger more imminent than those which menace young men, any temptations more seductive, any ruin more pitiable? Does she see any more susceptible of these influences than youth with their high spirits, superfluous energy and glowing passion? Does she see any victims which appeal more powerfully to her compassion than these sons and brothers in whose success and virtue are bound up the hopes and affections of thousands of parents, every one of whom cries to the world and to the church, "deal gently for my sake with the young man?"

2. But the church ought to deal with them, in the absence of other appliances to reach them. The church has few enough, far too few; but there are fewer elsewhere. Take business. What does it furnish? It deals with the young man. Not always gently either. It deals

with his youthful strength; with his clear and active brain; with his enterprise and energy. It uses these to build up trade and accumulate wealth. It deals, I say, not always gently. It is often exacting and severe. It often binds burdens too heavy for youthful shoulders. It often refuses leisure which health imperatively demands, and denies compensations which might furnish less temptation to crime. But I am not here to speak of these now. How does it deal with the young man morally? Does business take into the account, to any great extent, the fact that young men are moral and intellectual beings? How much leisure does it afford them for mental or religious culture? Alas, with the most charitable view of the case, with the noble exceptions clearly recognized, business presents a sad aspect in this regard. The maxim "*business is business*" is carried too far. What the *world* may think or do in this matter is not the question here; but to Christian men, who believe or profess to believe that religion belongs everywhere, business should be something more than business. How many Christian business men recognize in its contact opportunities for the exertion of Christian influence as well as for making money? How many see in their clerks something besides the hired arms or brains to carry on their trade? How many recognize them as beings with social instincts as well as with sharp wits; immortal souls as well as clear heads; susceptibilities to temptation as well as to self-interest; young men who are to fill a place in these democratic communities, to cast their votes, exert their influence, be each the centre of a greater or smaller circle, be fathers to train up children and perpetuate their own moral character and sentiments whatever they be? How many consider the influence which their position of employer gives them over the moral destiny of these youth; the power they may wield through the truly affectionate and confidential relations subsisting between them? How many concern themselves as to where their clerks go after business hours, what associations they form, whether they have a place of worship or not? How many of you business men, here to-day, are in the habit of asking the young men in your employ to accompany you to church, or to Bible class, or to prayer-meeting?

Take the community at large. *Its* influence, if exerted in this direction, must be chiefly confined to furnishing some counter attraction, moral, but not necessarily religious, to the attractions of the haunts of sin. And a great work can be done here, in which men of the most opposite religious theories, and men with no religion at all can unite. There, for instance, is the temperance question. There is a variety of views on the subject; but all agree that intemperance is an awful evil, and one which all moral and religious men are called on to resist and suppress by every possible means. *We* believe that the only effectual method of reforming a drunkard, or of keeping a man from becoming one, is to make him a Christian. That will reform in *all* respects. But we cannot bring the community to agree on this platform. Here then is one where all can unite, namely, in organizing some force to overbalance the attractions of the dram shop. It need not be distinctively religious, only free from vicious associations. The saloon keeper understands perfectly that not one young man in ten comes to his haunt originally to drink or in which to gamble. He wants a warm and pleasant room to sit down and chat with his companion; to read his evening paper, or it may be to procure a meal. So this minister of corruption proceeds to make provision for these natural and healthy cravings, that, through them, he may excite those unnatural and depraved desires, the satisfaction of which constitutes his chief source of profit. He furnishes his rooms tastefully and comfortably. He provides food of all kinds prepared to please the most fastidious palate. A small sum will secure a quiet and cosy retreat where the youth and his friends may pass an evening. But he furnishes the bar with its tempting array of liquors. He gathers there his array of well dressed and gentlemanly confederates who are always ready to challenge to drink, and to sneer at the principle which refuses. He has his licentious pictures to stimulate the passions, and abundant facilities for their gratification. And thousands of youths who went thither at first, only because they could find no other retreat, have come at last to frequent it for the gratification of the basest appetites, and have gone from its doors at last, hopeless, homeless drunkards.

Now suppose a community should say (and no individual with a shadow of moral sense could say otherwise), the rumseller takes an unfair advantage. He unites things which may just as well be separated. There is no necessity that all the light and comfort and retirement should be associated with liquor and licentiousness. Let us furnish these to the hundreds of poor young men who have no retreat but their offices and boarding houses. Let us build a house or hire a large suite of rooms. Let us have a suitable person employed to dispense proper refreshments at a reasonable price. Let us have a reading room furnished with the best papers and periodicals, and with a good library. Let us have a conversation room, where young men can chat or play their game of chess or backgammon. Let us have a ten pin alley, and even a smoking room. Would not this be in the interest of temperance as well as of many other virtues? Would it not keep scores of young men from the gin palaces? Could not society, independently of any religious views, easily inaugurate and carry out such a plan? It has been done, and has worked wonders. The slight approach towards it made by our Young Men's Christian Association, saying nothing now of the religious adjuncts, has proved what a strong, well organized effort might effect in this direction. And yet what has our communities of this character? What organized appliance have our cities anywhere to act upon young men? There I know are the Young Men's Associations, and they are good as far as they go; but they make provision chiefly for intellectual wants. Their libraries, and reading rooms, and lecture courses are doing a good work; but after all it is for the community at large, male and female, as well as for young men. There is a lower class of wants peculiar to young men, and to young men of a certain class, which will be supplied somehow, and which a proper effort may supply judiciously, without injury to the youth, and in a way to create wants and lead to associations of a higher character. If the moral and Christian part of the community do not supply them, the immoral part will.

3. But the church ought to deal with young men, *because she has the means.* She has organization. The community at large is not organized to carry out such efforts. Special organizations have to be made when such a movement is undertaken by it; and even then the *personal sympathy* and cooperation of individuals, except perhaps through their purses, is not secured. A moral movement agitated outside the church requires a good deal of time and effort to bring it into contact with men's minds, and to get them enlisted in it. It has to work principally upon individuals. But the moment a question of moral reform starts with the church, it works from the very first upon and through an organization. That is the reason why the agents

of all great benevolent enterprises and reform movements try first to get before the churches. The subject is presented to masses. It reaches the larger part of the community through their religious detachments, so to speak, and by the mouth of their chosen and respected religious instructors. The organization is already formed to discuss the question, to decide upon it, to raise means for carrying out the enterprise, to delegate men to represent this or that branch of the church in it. Added to this is the personal sympathy evoked. As a moral question it is brought home to the church on her own ground. If it concerns the salvation of men, every individual, as well as the church at large has to do with it. It appeals to him as a man and as a brother; to his prayers, to his pocket, to his effort.

The church has the wealth. I need only say, that the church represents by far the largest proportion of the money of our communities. Take our own city for instance, and count up our wealthiest men, and you will find that the most of them are not only members of congregations, but also members of churches.

4. The church ought to deal with young men, *because she represents the only restraining and reforming power.*

No reform that is not Christian in its essence is radical. No restraint that is not Christian is permanently effective. Other influences are partial in their operation. They modify one side of character. They protect it partially at one or two weak points. They touch the outward developments of the life merely; trying to regulate it from the circumference. This goes to the very seat of life, purges the fountain head of impulse and desire, creates a new man to do new works, and does not simply ingraft new works on the old character, putting the new piece into the old garment. This brings the thought and will into conformity with the law of Christ, and develops the man *as a whole*, makes him something, as well as restrains him from evil. Without this, who can say that any restraint will be effectual; that any memories will be sacred enough, any admonitions forcible enough, any associations attractive enough, any moral purpose strong enough to keep one pure? Alas, the shore of life is strewn so thickly with wrecks of youthful hope and promise, the annals of crime embrace so many youth of noble aims and high attainments, reared under the holiest influences of home and sanctuary, that we may well ask — who is safe?

While then, I would not discourage an effort at reform made in good faith by society, yet without any distinctively religious character, while I believe that many such efforts have done good in their sphere, I say distinctly, that their sphere is not large enough. Their influence does not reach deep enough. They help reform or restrain certain developments of the life; but they do not inaugurate any positive moral development. Nay, the very fact that many of them are forced, as a condition of their existence, to denude themselves of anything but the most general and vague religious character, makes them incapable of fostering any high moral development. To take the instance cited a few moments since. The community establishes a coffee room, or reading room, or resort of any kind for young men, without the vicious attractions of the fashionable restaurant or saloon. It does a good and laudable thing. Its influence is good as far as it goes, in keeping young men away from worse places. But the moral influence exerted, depends entirely upon these outside appliances. In other words, this institution keeps them from evil so long as they can have recourse to it, but does not implant within them a principle which, in the event of their being deprived of this privilege, would cause them to forego their comfort and recreation, rather than seek them amid debasing associations.

On this point then I am avaricious. I want the church to control all schemes of reform. I want them to originate in the church as their only legitimate source, so that in every effort put forth for the protection, or restoration, or training of youth, the gospel of Christ, the only power which can ever thoroughly regenerate individual or society, may be paramount: so that the effort may be not only a conservative but an aggressive force, winning youth to Christ as well as keeping them away from Satan, creating positive developments of character as well as securing simple safety or harmlessness, narrowing the boundaries of the devil's empire as well as keeping Christ's from infringement. For this reason I am anxious that instead of its being left for secular organizations to inaugurate such movements, the church should enlarge her Christian organizations so as to take in and sanctify every force that is requisite to meet the demands of the various characters with which sh ehas to deal.

And just at this point, I want to call your attention to a thought which bears especially upon our city churches.

It is commonly thought that the city is the fountain head of all vice, and with some reason I admit. Parents have a traditional horror of sending their sons into large cities. They think they are going into the very jaws of death and destruction. They draw a fearful picture of the gayeties and the temptations of city life. They look upon young men reared in cities with suspicion. They are inclined to regard them all as loose in morals, and as taking naturally to sin.

Now I do not believe that, as a rule, young men or any other men are worse in cities than elsewhere. Sin is pretty much the same thing, I apprehend, among grain and trees, as it is on sidewalks. Propensities just as vicious, passions just as furious and debased, exhibitions of vice quite as disgusting, more so, perhaps, because more coarse and pronounced, are to be seen in farming districts and in country villages as in cities. The appliances of vice are quite up to the proportion of the population in the former, both in quantity and in quality. A good deal of injustice is done the city in this respect. It is often said that a young man's ruin commences from the time he leaves his quiet country home and goes to the city. But the fact is that, in many cases, the city only completes what was well begun at home, begun in evenings spent in country grocery stores, and on the piazzas of village taverns.

But there is another aspect of this matter which would perhaps startle those who think that all piety and orthodoxy reside in the rural districts; and that is, that the city, *as it is*, affords far greater encouragements to well developed piety than the country; and that if the church were fully awake to her duty towards young men, and actually employing all the means afforded her by her wealth, organization and influence to shield, restrain, influence and reform them, the city would be the safest place on earth for a youth. If the city is the stronghold of vice, it is in the church's power to make it the stronghold of virtue. For it is admitted that, in other respects, the city affords superior advantages. Young men leave the country store and come thither if they desire to learn business on a large scale. They are obliged to seek the city for large literary opportunities. The great popular literary attractions seldom move out of the track of the cities. Here the pulse of life beats quicker. Men live faster. Thought is more energetic and prompt. The same is in a measure true of religious life. It develops more activity, more benevolence. It invests religious instruction with more attractions, and throws more life and power into social worship. Go into such a prayer meeting, for instance, as you can find in scores of churches in our large cities, where the large numbers present augment the sympathy of each with the common object, where thoughtful, practical, energetic men pour into the common treasury streams of fresh, living thought, where the singing is an inspiration, and say what you will, a man will be stirred and stimulated as he cannot be in the thin assemblies of too many country churches, where the minister is chiefly depended on to give interest to the meeting, where the singing is faint and slow. I know God is often in the one place as in the other. I know there is true religious life there, and that souls are converted there. But so long as men remain human, their piety will not be insensible to such influences. So too, the influences of the city churches tend more to develop young men. My impression is that in country districts age is a prime qualification for responsibility; young men are kept back, and not expected to bear a prominent part in religious services until later in life. With us, it is part of our creed to educate young men by responsibility. We love to hear them speak or pray, not only because they bring us good and fresh and profitable thoughts, but because we know that these exercises are developing them into strong men for the future leaders of the church. Not only so, but our larger religious machinery, the wider sphere of our activity, furnish places for them to work. We must depend largely upon them to carry on our mission schools, and to carry out other practical schemes of benevolence. Under these influences, I say, they develop faster, and as I think better. As a rule, the young man of a city church is more capable, more efficient, than one of the same age and of equal natural abilities in a rural district.

But then these influences do not reach the class of unconverted youth directly. They have no interest in prayer meetings, little in sermons. This is the plain question before us then:

III. *How shall the church deal with the Absaloms:* the erring youth or those of no religious bias, the careless and pleasure loving? *There is such a class.* Are you surprised at my stating a fact which seems self evident? I state it because it seems to have been practically forgotten. Some men frame their schemes of reform on the principle that every one must be appealed to by the same influences which appeal to them. For in-

stance, when it is proposed to furnish, under Christian supervision, certain innocent appliances which may counterbalance the attractions of the saloon, and perhaps lead to the exercise of some more distinctively religious influence, we are flatly told by some that there is no need of recreation. Youth are on the brink of the grave, and should find enjoyment in singing psalms. Others tell us there is recreation enough in the contemplation of the heavenly bodies, and of the beauties of nature, and that these ought to satisfy the soul without its having recourse to lower joys. Now you and I like to sing psalms. They are suggestive to us of many rich and comforting thoughts. Some of you can find sufficient enjoyment in the beauties of nature, not only because God has opened your eyes to see him in all things, but because study and knowledge have prepared your mind to discern and appreciate the wonders of creation. I don't think you particularly loved to sing psalms before Christ touched your heart. And the practical point we have got to meet, and meet as Christians and with Christian methods is, that there is a large class that cannot be appealed to by the beauties of nature and the charms of literature, and the glory of the starry heavens. Have we anything to do with these? Just as indubitably as David's army had to do with the erring Absalom. And we have got to deal gently with them too; not force them upon the procrustean bed of our methods, and give them their choice of these or none. If the church says to these unconverted, careless ones, "If you will not come to our prayer meetings, if you will not listen to our sermons, we have done our duty and cleared our skirts, and you may go on to perdition as fast as you please," I say the church is awfully in error. Her skirts, are in that event, soaked with the blood of ruined youth, and it cries aloud against her from the ground.

What are we to do then? If the church has a duty to this class, has she also means to discharge it? Is it in her power to make the city the best place for irreligious as well as for pious youth? I say, yes. But she will be obliged to enlarge her scheme of work. She must sanctify new forces to this end, if she has to take them out of the devil's hand. She must institute new attractions, under her own control, to draw youth within the sphere of her influence, and to hold them when drawn. She must employ forces with a view merely to restrain from worse influences, until she can bring direct religious influences to bear. Without compromising principle one iota, abstaining from the very appearance of evil, she is nevertheless to press into her service everything that she can separate from low associations, everything that will enhance her own social attractions, everything which will amuse, interest, instruct, to keep these away from the palaces of hell, and to draw them into contact with the influences of the gospel. The wisdom of Christianity is shown in its dealing with men as they are. In reaching them at their own level; and the church will best show her wisdom by not trying to be wiser than her Lord. The mountain will not go to Mahomet, and Mahomet must go to the mountain. We have a variety of characters to deal with, and must use a variety of means. Gather such a band of youth together, and preach to them that they ought to be satisfied with the beauties of nature, or with books, or the like, and you simply drive them the faster from religious influences, and cut every tie between you. Here is one young man who loves books. Let the church give him books. Let him know that he receives this high and pure pleasure from the hand of Christianity. Here is another that loves pictures. Let Christian art adorn the walls, and Christian liberality pay the price. But here is another of a lower grade of culture. Not vicious, not specially inclined to dissipation, but finding little interest in books or pictures. Throw him among these higher influences, of course, for they will insensibly educate him; but if a checker board or a game of dominoes will attract him, and keep him for an evening away from the liquor saloon or the theatre, pray tell me why Christian hands should not furnish him these, and a pleasant, quiet place in which to play his innocent game, where no profanity greets his ears, where no bar presents its seductions. Another loves music; why should not Christian liberality furnish him the gratification of this taste, and Christian hands and voices join with him in swelling the harmony in which his heart delights?

It is, of course, impossible for me to go into details here, but the general principle I think is clear. It seems to me that the only way in which the church can reach any large proportion of these young men, is by the judicious union of attractive and direct influences; by bringing under her own control and using all those appliances which appeal to the social instinct, to the taste, to the intellect, to the necessity for recreation, freeing them from debasing associations, and thereby drawing the unconverted youth within the range of direct religious influences. She must be content to keep them out of the hands of evil for the time, if she cannot fully commit them to piety. But then, let it be clearly understood that these things are to be under the control of religion. That the *salvation* of the young men is the great end toward which these are only means. The moment our Young Men's Christian Associations, to which we must chiefly look to carry out this plan, let their rooms become mere lounging places; the moment the prayer meeting is dropped; the moment the young men cease to be on the watch for opportunities to speak the word of religious counsel, that moment they are no longer the allies of the church; they will have become no better than clubs. I want to say to the young men of our own association who have so boldly and, thus far, so successfully carried out this theory, you must guard yourselves here. The Troy Association has drawn the eyes of the church throughout a large part of the country upon itself by its course in this matter. It is thought by many a bold experiment. By many it is openly denounced. Many predict that the result will be the ruin instead of the salvation of young men. If you would silence and convert your opponents, if you would convert the wavering into enthusiastic supporters of your policy, guard well the religious side of your work. Infuse the gospel spirit into everything. Strictly enforce the rules which Christian prudence lays down for the use of means and attractions not distinctively religious. Let the word *Christian* be in the largest letters on your sign. Remember your great object, the duty thrown upon you by the nature of the case, thrown upon you by similarity of age, by congeniality of taste and pursuits, thrown upon you by the church, thrown upon you by Christ; the church's head, is the *salvation*, not the entertainment of the young men. You use these appliances to entertain, only that thereby you may bring other forces to bear, which may make them Christians, add their power to the various churches of the community, and unite them with you in the work of saving others. The moment you forget this, Ichabod will be written upon your banners, and the cause of Christ receive a blow which all the good you have heretofore accomplished can scarcely heal.

The practical working of this theory is the best answer to its opponents. We have this answer among us to-day, and I am thankful from my inmost heart that the Young Men's Christian

Association is to-day, what it was not two years ago, among the great religious forces of our city. Those who have opposed its later proceedings have some stubborn facts to get round. These facts demonstrate this: that since the Young Men's Christian Association inaugurated the policy of *attracting* youth to its head-quarters, its *distinctively religious force has increased ten-fold.* As one evidence of this, the city missionary says, "since we entered upon our present plan, a larger number of young men than ever before have been brought to sympathize with me and my work, are ready to sit up with the sick, to visit the needy, to labor for the spiritual good of their fellows. Our rooms have resulted in increasing the effective force of spiritual co-laborers with me, more than *ten-fold.*" Last month, the daily prayer meeting from twelve to one, was attended by an average of twenty-two daily, mostly young persons, and generally conducted by young men converted under the agency of the association. Some of you remember the old noonday prayer meeting, and to such I need say nothing as to the contrast. The call for this noonday meeting was signed by about fifty young men. The call itself was drawn and circulated by a young man who, six months ago, came to our city penniless, was made to feel at home in our rooms, was furnished with employment by the agencies of the association, came to the weekly prayer meeting, was converted, and is now counted among our most earnest Christian workers. Young men are being converted through this agency. I give you one instance out of a number. A young man visited the rooms on Thursday night, and was invited with others down to the young men's prayer meeting. He went, and was deeply interested, and immediately after the meeting returned to the parlor, and was seen earnestly studying a Bible at one of the reading tables. At the hour of closing, some of the Christian young men accompanied him home, and urged upon him the subject of personal religion. They followed him up for two or three days, until he gave his heart to God; and he has since been an active co-laborer with the young men in the work of the association.

One more incident. A young man came to one of the members of this church sometime since, saying, "I came to the city two years ago. I was a member of a church at home; but here, no man seemed to care for my soul. I have neglected my duty, have sought for no church home; but I was attracted to your rooms. I went to the association prayer meeting. My heart was stirred, and I became ashamed of my neglect and inconsistency; and now I want to know when your next communion season is, that I may give my letter to your pastor."

I could give you others, but these speak volumes for the value of this policy; and, from the bottom of my heart this morning, I say God bless the Young Men's Christian Association, and pledge them my poor efforts and influence, and prayers to help forward the work so nobly begun.

I know not where to stop. My heart is so full that it seems as if I could spend the day on this theme. But I must stop, and, in conclusion I say, first to the church, accept frankly the responsibility which God throws on you in the persons of these young men. You are the appointed agency, the proper agency, and the only agency to save and restrain and protect them. You cannot shirk it, especially as city churches. Into these centres of trade and education God pours the young men, and he asks you and me this morning if we are ready for them; if, while business and education are multiplying their facilities, the gospel of Christ, represented by the churches, is multiplying its facilities to make the city the *best place* for the education of young men in virtue. He asks these churches if there is nothing significant, no message to her in the concentration of the mass of our young men and the mass of Christian culture, organized power, and wealth, at one point? Have these things no relation to each other? Yes, brethren, they have. There is no evading it. The finger of Providence points unswervingly to these city churches as the great sources of Christian influence upon young men. Let us not fail to hear these voices. The ten thousand appliances of vice, confronting the church with brazen defiance, or with devilish ingenuity and secresy sapping the foundations of manly honor and integrity, call to us, deal gently with the young man. Fathers and mothers, the yearnings of whose hearts you read full easily in your love for your own sons, whose happiness, whose very lives are bound up in the honor and prosperity of these sons and brothers, call to us from their distant homes in quiet villages, and on the open farm lands, call to us with agonizing earnestness — deal gently for our sakes with the young man. Our community, our country, calls to us. Oh, when I look upon society and see what characters ride rampant there, when I look at government and see the awful corruption festering there, when I see how men in power, from the chief magistrate of the nation down to the humblest postmaster, will sell their souls for party, and betray their country to its enemies through lust of power, or something else, God knows what; when I see drunkenness holding high carnival in the nation's capitol, reeling in the seat of the President, and retailing its maudlin declamation before a sickened country from Washington to Chicago, I can only turn to God and the future. Our only hope is in the work of the Christian church through all its agencies, social, ecclesiastical and educational, moulding out of the glorious material so abundantly at its disposal, a band of men who shall convert the seats of power into seats of righteousness, and make government and purity synonymous terms. The young men themselves appeal to us. This mass of intelligence, clear wit, energy, tact, education; these noble brows on which God has set the seal of power; these frank, manly, generous natures, these enthusiastic impulses, all speak to us, saying, deal gently with us, and teach us by the power of Christian love how to use our power; they speak to us, and warn us against letting so much power and energy and culture be turned against us, or left to hang as a drag on our wheels. And Christ speaks to the church, Christ who loves these young men, Christ who died for these young men; Christ who from his seat of glory at the Father's right hand, yearns over these young men, Christ is calling to his church to-day, to you, to me, to all the pastors and congregations of this city, "*take care of them, take care of them, deal gently for* MY *sake with the young men.*"

Christian young men, you have heard the call, and in some sort are obeying it. In proportion as you have not feared to use the range of gospel agencies, in proportion as your love has been kindled for the souls of these youths, and your hands and tongues have been devoted to this end, God has blessed you. Go on as you have begun. Go on, not defiantly, but firmly, boldly, prudently. Dare to be singular, if it will compass your end. Take the word of God as your highest authority. Use no means that is not sanctioned by it. Use none of doubtful expediency, but enlarge the range of your agencies. Wrest from the devil attractions which belong to you rather than to him. Leaven them. Separate them from the debasing associations with which sin has indentified them, and in the name of Christ your Master, set up your banners, rally your forces and join the churches in their work of salvation.

And you, unconverted young men, one word to you. For your own souls' sake, for the sake of your best interests, for the sake of the parents who love and hope in you, for the sake of your country, for Christ's sake, deal gently with yourselves. Remember, the only true manhood is Christian manhood. No restraints which the church can throw round you will ensure your safety against temptation; no strength of resolution on your part will keep you pure, if you be not the children of Christ. Come to Jesus. Come this very morning. Come and learn of him. He will deal very gently with you. His yoke is easy, his burden is light. The life he gives you is full of the highest impulses and of the purest enjoyments — a living spring of water — and the eternal rewards he promises are such as eye hath not seen, nor ear heard, nor the heart of man conceived.

THOUGHTS

FOR THE CLERGY

ON THE

AMUSEMENT QUESTION.

THOUGHTS FOR THE CLERGY

ON

THE AMUSEMENT QUESTION.

As pastors, we can no longer evade this question. Our people are hearing, reading, and being influenced by discussions of the subject in various quarters. Obviously, we must not let our congregations form their conclusions on so important a matter, independently of their chosen spiritual guides. The word of each pastor will carry with it, in most cases, a weight which can attach to no other's word. Let us see to it that we separate ourselves, as much as possible, from prejudice in our examination of this question. Let us face the facts fairly, and inquire what provision is furnished by the gospel to meet them. We have nothing to do with any other consideration. Whether the gospel principles and methods applicable to this case appear to us safe or unsafe, we have no right to advocate any other. We have no right to be silent.

What are the facts?

1. *The youth, as a class, are vitally important to the church and to the state.* Our work as Christian teachers reaches beyond our own generation. We owe to the future the proper training of the men and women who are to mould its destinies. The present youth are the future leaders of church and state. How they shall lead them, depends very much upon us. These truths are self-evident.

2. *They are exposed to peculiar dangers calling for special effort on their behalf.*

Special efforts are being made to ruin them. The self-interest of vice is interested in this work; for to youth its appliances look chiefly for support. As one has happily expressed it, "Age has few passions to which profligacy can appeal; and the proselytism of decrepitude and years are enlistments of little value." The withdrawal of young men from the rolls of the intemperate and licentious, would leave two-thirds of the drinking saloons and brothels bankrupt. The passions to which these appliances appeal are such as are most active and dangerous in youth. They offer the freedom and license which youth loves. They throw off the shackles which youth hates. Our cities and villages swarm with traps set expressly for them. Thousands are freely expended to invest the bar room and the gambling hell with the cozy attractions of the parlor. The harlot's palace opens wide its doors. The public ball room displays its fascinations. Dissipation draws round itself the attractions of wealth and taste and fashion, and in its splendid club rooms secures for itself the pleasures which expediency forbids it to seek more publicly. Vice literally flaunts its banners in the face of the public. But a few days since I saw from my window a banner carried through the streets, blazoned with the name and attractions of one of the vilest fashionable groggeries in the city, and preceded by the music of a drum and fife. The snug retreat, known only to the initiated few, where licentiousness and drunkenness are secluded, and thousands lost and won, was never more popular than now. Practiced decoys lie in wait for the daughters of our families, and the whirl of general society in which so many of them, at a tender age, are madly revolving night after night, is no poor preparation for the fatal success of these wiles. Young girls, who come from quiet country homes to seek employment, cast adrift on these surging tides of life without a friend or an adviser, readily fall victims to the wiles of young seducers whose social position ensures their security. In a certain city, I was informed not long since, of one keeper of a fashionable brothel who had removed her trade, because it was too largely usurped by victims of this class to render it any longer profitable. Young men, too, are coming to the cities in crowds, to engage in business or study. They must have society and recreation; and the votaries of vice are sparing neither pains nor expense to give them abundance of both, fraught with ruin to soul and body.

Without going outside of our special sphere as pastors, viewing this subject solely with reference to the youth of our congregations, as, in common with others subjected to these and other temptations, *what ought to be our influence in arresting and counteracting these evils?*

It ought to be second to none but parental influence. If the name pastor mean anything, our position as the chosen religious teachers of congregations ought to give us free access to every household in our flocks, and the strongest influence over the youth whose moral training we directly or indirectly shape. We ought to be not only *respected* and *reverenced*, but so loved as to be the familiar advisers and confidants of the youth of our charges. Our word ought, next to the parents', to have weight in turning them from improper courses and associations, and in keeping them from such. Moreover, our influence ought not to be merely restrictive and admonitory. We should be sufficiently in sympathy with them, familiar enough with the demands of their age and with the best means of satisfying them, to be able to offer positive suggestions respecting their employments, recreations, society, reading, and the like. If we sustain proper relations to the youth of our charges, they will be as likely to refer such questions to us, as matters of theology or practical morality.

Now, the question of the amusements of our youth is as good a test question in this matter as we need ask. *What, then, is the influence of the clergy at large in regulating the diversions of the youth?*

I appeal to the experience of the mass of ministers, not with the few *special friends* and admirers, which most of them have among the young people of their congregations, but with the *mass of the youth.* I appeal to those judicious, far-seeing Christians, who are wont to observe carefully the tendencies of society, *if this influence is not a comparative nullity.* In a question which, perhaps, as much as any other, concerns the welfare of our youth, which has the most vital relations to the attractions of home, which will enter, whether we may think it right or not, into the considerations which influence the choice or rejection of a religious life; at a point which the ministers of vice are fortifying most strongly, wresting the best diversions to themselves, striving to make them peculiarly their own, and to invest them permanently with associations which shall exclude them from Christian homes; here, I say, the Christian church, the appointed regulator and instructor in the ethics of amusement, is, to a great extent, *at open issue with her own intelligent youth, and practically powerless to execute her own decrees.*

It is well for us as ministers, to look this fact squarely in the face, and to call things by their right names. How many pastors are in the confidence of their youth with respect to the amusements of the latter? Is not the fact rather that there is a tacit antagonism recognized between the youth and the clergy on this subject, an antagonism growing, too, every year less tacit and more avowed? Can it be denied that a very large proportion of our youth regard their ministers as the foes to recreation, and would sooner think of consulting them on any subject than on this? Is it not the fact that while presbyteries and conferences and conventions pass long and stringent resolutions on the subject of dancing and on the use of cards and billiards, multitudes of Christian families practice dancing; scores of them may be found playing whist at their own firesides, and scores more with their billiard rooms fitted up in their own houses? It will not answer to say that those who practice these things are backslidden in heart and worldly minded, and that, if they were truly Christ's children, they would neither practice nor desire them. This is begging the whole question at issue, and moreover is flatly contradicted by facts. Many of those who engage in these recreations are among the most devoted, enlightened, faithful members and even ministers of our churches. Is it not the fact, again, that the pastors of these individuals would be very much at a loss to administer discipline in such cases? Do they not know that any attempt at authoritative interference would be regarded as trenching upon individual rights of conscience, and would send scores of active and faithful members to other communions? The truth is, and there is no shirking it, that, in the cities especially, in the largest and most powerful churches, the clergy are practically brought to a stand in this matter. They do not and cannot control it. A vast mass of enlightened Christian sentiment is against their attempts to enforce the traditional church doctrines on this subject. Their people pay little or no heed to the official utterances of church assemblies. Many of them treat them with ridicule. There is no denying these facts. Hundreds of pastors are painfully impressed with them. The church's position in this matter is most humiliating.

What then is the course of the clergy?

Some of them are more than half persuaded that the more liberal view of their people is correct. They fully sympathize, perhaps, with that view, yet they remain silent. They cannot conscientiously reprove; they refuse to come boldly forward and define their position for fear of awakening prejudice, or for fear their views may be misunderstood or misconstrued. In short they think it is not safe. And yet, all the while, the initiated in the congregation know pretty well the general drift of their minister's sentiments;

that, though he says little, he winks a tacit encouragement to many indulgences which far overstep the bounds of ancient orthodoxy. But is *this* safe? Is it safe or honorable for the church to be impotent to carry out her own dogmas? Is it safe for her to be under the charge of inconsistency from the world because her statute books and the practice of her members are at open variance? Is it safe for the views of an influential Christian teacher to be known only generally and vaguely, that his church and the world may draw undue license therefrom? If he is convinced that the church has been mistaken in this matter, and has in past years committed herself to undue stringency, is it safe to let the error remain untouched, and going on working its pernicious consequences? If the gospel teaches a larger liberty, a broader conception of Christian living and Christian enjoyment than the church has preached, has that minister who conscientiously believes the fact any right to withhold the truth because he deems it unsafe, and to let a falsehood (as he believes) gain currency and power, and forfeit moreover the attraction presented to a sinful world by his more cheering and liberal conception of Christ's teachings? Not safe! Will not God take care of his truth? Doubtless men will misconstrue it. Doubtless they will wrest the preaching of gospel liberty to the confirmation of worldly license. But the greater the danger of this, the more reason why the truth, the *whole truth*, should be proclaimed loudly, boldly, distinctly, frequently. When the water is first let into a reservoir, it is apt to be very muddy; but that is no reason why the reservoir should remain dry forever. The water will settle by and by, and the whole people be refreshed. If there is truth in these more liberal views of amusement, it is in vain for religious newspapers to shirk the discussion of the question. It is in vain for influential ministers to beg young men's Christian conventions not to raise it. It is in vain for the pulpit to preserve a discreet silence. The thing will out. The truth will stay swathed in no cave in the rock. The things that have been spoken in the ear in closets will be proclaimed upon the house tops. The Christian public will the sooner attain correct views on this subject through free discussion. If the thing be not of God, it will sooner come to nought through this process than through any other. But by their love for souls, and by their sworn loyalty to God and truth, let the clergy run the sword of the Spirit through and through this matter, that the world may know the truth and detect the falsehood.

It is confessed by some that they have given the subject no attention. They have accepted the traditions of the church as they found them, have preached and have tried to enforce them, or else have settled down upon the assumption that the matter is of minor importance. I simply ask if this is justifiable in view of the facts; in view of the contradictory position of the church on this subject; in view of the important part which amusements must play in the education of youth; in view of their great and patent abuses; in view of the point urged in these discourses that many of the popular diversions of the day may be wrested from the devil's hands and turned to good purpose in keeping the young from evil influences and associations?

Some *positively refuse* to consider the question under any new aspect. It is settled, once and for all. The books are balanced, shut and sealed. The wisdom of a past generation exhausted the question. Its dictum is to be received as gospel. Little needs to be said here. Such declarations demand the utmost stretch of Christian charity. They betray an ignorance which, in a popular teacher, is unpardonable, and a blind acquiescence in the conclusions of the past which is pitiable.

The truth, moreover, is not promoted, *in any direction*, by abusing those of more liberal views on this question. The man who conscientiously believes them wrong, and boldly says so, and does not simply declaim against them but opposes them by fair argument drawn from scripture, is to be honored. I would there were more such. But it will not in the least tend to conciliate favor for the more stringent aspect of the question, for its advocates to cast slurs upon the sincerity and piety of those who differ from them, to announce them as corrupters of youth, enemies of the church, underminers of pure religion, and the like. The day for this has gone by. The best men may differ even on this question, which some think so firmly settled; and the liberal view of this subject is supported by too many shining names in the Christian ministry, by too large a mass of Christian devotion and consistency and learning and intelligence, to entitle such assertions to any notice whatever. The want of Christian charity which leads one public teacher to asperse his brother's Christian consistency and purity of motive upon such grounds, is at least as reprehensible as the holding of liberal sentiments on dancing or billiards.

Once more. The pulpit, in some places, though alive to the importance of the subject, is holding sternly by its old, stringent views. It is laying down the law authoritatively, decrying as sinful all but a very limited allowance of amusements.

The results of this policy so long and so thoroughly tried, are before us. With all this preaching, the prevalence and variety of amusements steadily increases. Year after year such utterances of the pulpit fall with less weight. Year after year the character and standing of those who openly set them at defiance renders it more and more difficult to back them by discipline. The clergy are not gaining ground with the youth. Hundreds of the latter, repelled by this teaching, are tearing themselves away from the churches of their fathers, to unite with folds where a more liberal gospel is preached. A prominent merchant of the Methodist church, a man whose name is known in both hemispheres, wrote me, not more than a month ago, "the teachings of my own church on this subject have had the effect to drive nearly my whole family into the Protestant Episcopal church."

It is sometimes said: "Let them go. We are better without such. We do not want members who will not relinquish these suspected amusements. We do not want half way Christians, conformed to the world, trying to hold fast to pleasure and secure heaven at the same time." But such statements do not fairly represent the case. Again, the whole question is begged. Many of those who refuse to conform to the churches dicta on these subjects care nothing whatever for the amusements in question. The matter is entirely one of principle. They leave our churches, not because conscience is relaxed, but because it is acutely sensitive, and because they would keep it unsullied. The above method of putting the case assumes that all the conscience is on one side; that, while it operates strongly to condemn, it cannot possibly operate to approve. Many of these persons resort to other communions, because they are too honest to compromise with conscience; because they cannot see these questions in the light in which their own churches present them; and rather than go to God's altars with even an implied falsehood upon their consciences, or embrace the alternative of remaining outside of Christ's fold, they will sever life-long ties, entwined with some of their dearest and tenderest recollections, and go alone with their conscience and their God to altars where no such tests are imposed. And in these new associations they bear themselves with all Christian fidelity. They bring forth rich fruits of grace. They walk humbly and consistently with God. They are exemplary fathers and mothers. They are liberal in their gifts to the cause of Christ, and active in promoting schemes to advance it. Our churches have been driving away such men and women as these who would have been their ornaments and bulwarks, because they have sought unduly to constrain Christian conscience on these subjects.

Worse than this. This course is keeping youth away from *all* church communions; away from Christ. Few pastors have not received this answer, when urging young persons to come to the Savior. "If I become a Christian, I must be very solemn. I must repress my lightness of heart. I must relinquish all my cherished enjoyments." Admit that these views are greatly exaggerated, as doubtless they are, the question forces itself upon us, *why do we meet such views so often?* Why are they so generally prevalent among our youth? Why does the immense amount of preaching, forcible, eloquent preaching, on the comforts and joys of a Christian life produce, seemingly, so little impression upon them? Why is it that they persist in regarding *Christian* joy as a sickly, stunted thing, and religion as the enemy of all light and hilarity and taste and freedom?

Is all this result of native depravity? I cannot believe it. I cannot dissociate a large measure of this most lamentable result from the old teaching and practice of the church on the subject of recreation. It is of no use to preach to ardent, active youth, that Christianity is a religion of joy, unless they see some joy brought out of it besides mere smiles and a class of recreations which to them as a class are insipid. To them *Christian* cheerfulness appeals as being less cheerful than any other kind; as a sort of mild, repressed gayety, from which their quick sensibilities and stirring blood revolts. They feel that in the church they must be cheerful only in the way the church directs. Those ministers, they reason, can be very cheerful, and even laugh uproariously over a discussion on decrees; but what do I care for decrees? Those elderly Christians can be cheerful in a quiet conversation on politics or on the church. But if I want to be cheerful in a merry dance in proper society and at proper hours, if I want to go to my friend's billiard table and play a quiet game, if I want to make merry over a few hits of backgammon, or give my energy full vent in rolling ten-pins for an hour, I am a heathen and a publican and unfit for the society of Christians.

As already observed, these views are doubtless greatly exaggerated by the young. Yet does not the state of the case warrant us in asking carefully and prayerfully if there is no connection between the stringent dogmas of the church on the subject of recreation, and the general suspicion of religion which characterizes the mass of unconverted youth?

Be this as it may, the case is narrowed down to this. Of all the subjects naturally under the church's supervision, there is not one in which her influence is less than in this. She neither represses nor regulates. One of two courses she must pursue if she would escape the stigma of impotency. Either she must reassert her old dogmas, and back them by the severest discipline, or she must modify them, and openly commit herself to a larger liberty. Is she prepared for the first of these courses? Is she prepared, first of all, to defend it from God's Word. Every other defense is worthless here. Is she ready to cut off remorselessly the man or the woman, the youth or the maid who dances, however properly and modestly? Is she ready to expel or suspend every minister who shall roll a ten-pin ball, or while away an hour with chess or backgammon? Is she ready to lay violent hands upon every member who fingers a card or handles a cue, or strikes a croquet ball? If so, I tremble for the results of the experiment. She will pause before she undertakes this course. Or will she openly confess to undue stringency in the past, and write a new motto upon her banners—"More abundant life?" Here what seems a formidable objection is often preferred with great confidence. Grant that these more liberal views are correct, still public sentiment is not yet such as to make it safe to promulgate them. The argument, both in its character and result, very strongly resembles that which used to be such a favorite with the advocates of slavery. The negro is not fit for freedom. It recoiled on those who advanced it. Who made the negro unfit for freedom but those who held him in bondage until his imbruted nature ceased to prize or to desire liberty? Similarly I say, if there is such a state of public sentiment, *why is it so?* How came this thing there? Who is responsible for a state of sentiment in the church which makes it inexpedient to declare the plain teachings of Christ on *any* subject? There can be but one answer. The responsibility lies between the church and the world, and the world surely has not done it. The church herself has made this sentiment, has created the factitious conscience, has awakened the morbid sensibility, by preaching on this subject a theory which shrivels at the touch of Christ, and which she has clearly shown her inability to carry into practice. And the fact that such a sentiment exists, so far from calling for silence, is the strongest of all reasons why the church should speak out with a voice of thunder, and set herself right with the vast mass of conscience which she so powerfully influences.

Would you then, says one, free this matter entirely from the restraints of the church? By no means. On the contrary, I am calling upon the church to regain influence which she has forfeited. I am pleading for a *regulation* of these things by the church which does not now exist. Indulgence is going too far in the church itself. But from her present stand-point on this question, the church is, from the very nature of the case, almost powerless to regulate. Assuming that the recreations in question are evil and only evil, she *must not* regulate. That would be compromising. She must *crush*. Hence the matter resolves itself into a war of extermination on both sides. Either these forms of amusement must be exterminated from the church, or they must get the upper hand of the church's statutes, in which case the church has no law for them. She has only provided for destroying them; and failing in this, must stand and see them run riot in her very courts.

I would not have the church compromise one hair's-breadth with sin. Better that she should err in excessive stringency. But I would have her gain a new vantage ground *by being simply true*, and not proclaiming unmixed evil, where evil and good are blended in liberal proportions. By not undertaking the task of *extermination*, where her duty is that of *discrimination*. The moment she begins upon the principle of *analyzing* these mixed elements, casting only the bad away, and using, developing and enjoying the good, that moment she mounts to a point from which she can regulate *any* matter which falls under her jurisdiction. And to be thus true, she must go direct to Christ. His word and example are conclusive, and we may safely preach what we find there. Do we find any such principle of repression as the church has preached for years past? No; we find abuse condemned, and use allowed and approved. The Savior is at the hilarious merry-making of the marriage, contributing to the festivity. His own parable is on record, bidding men put the gospel into all the forms and developments of life, to refine and fit them for human enjoyment. The long list of exceptions with which men are forbidden to bring the gospel leaven into contact has been added by men, not by Christ. He was condemned for the very same reason for which hundreds condemn a so called liberal Christian to-day; because he used the world which other men used, and thought it not necessary to abstain from use because others abused. These teachings are there if anything is there. They are for all time. The conditions of no age can justify Christians in refusing to preach and to apply them just as they stand. Nine-tenths of the really sinful indulgence over which the church is mourning to-day, is simply because of the failure to do this faithfully. Because good men have been startled by the magnitude and power of evil, and have been too timid to meet it with methods which seemed so slow, and which even gave room for the charge of compromise. In being wiser than her Lord, the church has drawn the reins too tightly, and the results speak for themselves. Much is said about expediency; and

Paul's words about meat offending his brother, have been saddled with more burdens than any ten other passages of scripture; but after all, the result proves simply this, that it is always most expedient to follow Christ implicitly.

I would, moreover, that the church in dealing with this question, would consent to meddle less with its details, and leave them more where they properly belong, with the individual conscience. No one man can decide these things for another. No man has a right to insist that his standard of expediency shall be his brother's. Where God's law is explicit, both are bound alike. When it throws a decision upon conscience, neither has a right to complain if the paths diverge. Both paths may not be right, but to his own Master shall each traveler stand or fall.

The church, indeed, can do better than to busy herself with such details, or, to speak more correctly, she can deal with them much more successfully by shifting her point of power from the circumference to the centre. Her duty in this case will be very much simplified and lightened, if she will give more attention to the *springs* of Christian life, to the conformity of the *heart* to the mind and will of Christ, to fostering an enthusiastic devotion to him. Then these details and distinctions will mostly take care of themselves. The church has lacked faith in the regulative power of this principle, and has sought to supply its assumed defects by innumerable special provisions; and the consequent tendency of this course has been to fetter Christian individuality, and to insist that love to Christ should express itself only in such modes as the church might prescribe. Hence the sentiment often expressed, a true Christian will have no taste for these things. But here again the whole question is begged. You do not know, you cannot know what affinities a Christian life may develop. All that you can with any confidence assert is the general fact that he will love all that is good, acceptable, perfect, and hate all that is essentially evil. As to other matters, things whose moral value arises entirely from circumstances, a love to Christ as sincere and as ardent as yours, may lead him in a direction the very opposite of yours. Therefore it will be more in the interest of a true Christian individuality, of a higher and more generous Christian manhood, for the church to throw the soul more on its love to Christ as the great regulative principle. Let her probe the hearts committed to her, deeply for this. Let her strengthen this sentiment by every possible safeguard. Let her urge her members earnestly to higher attainments in this, and her difficulties in the regulation of the amusement question, and of every similar question will, in a great degree, disappear. Her courts will be full of the richest developments of grace, the most varied activities, the most glorious examples of that wondrous unity in diversity which Christianity alone displays.

Might not the church, moreover, profitably ask herself if there be not a positive duty toward these much abused things, as well as a privilege of letting them alone? If a thing has good in it, does Christ teach that our duty to it is discharged in letting it alone for the sake of the evil mixed with it? That is the easier way, I know. It is a good deal easier to throw overboard good and evil together, than to separate them carefully and to develop the good into a power. But if easier, is it better? I cannot avoid quoting just here the exquisite words of Trench on the Marriage at Cana, as bringing out clearly our Savior's example on this point: "We need not wonder to find the Lord of life at that festival; for he came to sanctify all life, its times of joy, as its times of sorrow; *and all experience tells us that it is times of gladness, such as this was now, which especially need such a sanctifying power, such a presence of the Lord.* In times of sorrow the sense of God's presence comes most naturally out; in these it is in danger to be forgotten. He was there, and by his presence struck the key-note to the whole future tenor of his ministry. He should not be as another Baptist, to withdraw himself from the common paths of men, a preacher in the wilderness; but his should be at once a harder and a higher task, to mingle with and purify the common life of men, to witness for and bring out the glory which was hidden in its every relation." To the same purpose are the pertinent words of Aiford: "To endeavor to evade the work which he has appointed for each man, by refusing the bounty to save the trouble of seeking the grace, is an attempt which must ever end in degradation of the individual motives and in social demoralization, whatever present apparent effects may follow its first promulgation."

"A terrible responsibility you are taking on yourself," say some to the writer. "Youth are going to perdition on your authority, pleading your word and example as a Christian minister." I have only to say I fear not to meet such before the highest of all tribunals. If any man shall, after carefully reading these four discourses, say that they give his worldly heart full license to indulge its will, I tell him to his face, he is either a fool or a hypocrite. Not proudly, I trust, but in humble reliance upon him for whose sake every line has been penned, I bow my shoulders to every morsel of responsibility which the utterance of these truths involves. No youth will go to perdition on their authority. If he shall infer the right to abuse from a plea for moderate Christian use, his perdition be on his own head. The truth I have uttered shall condemn him. If I err, God will bring this thing to nought: and I, who have erred in good faith, and with an honest conscience, shall be dealt with by a tender Savior as lovingly and leniently as I believe he will deal with those who, with equal sincerity and zeal, may possibly have erred in so presenting to youth a gospel of light and joy and freedom, as to make some of them prefer the risk of perdition to embracing it.

www.ingramcontent.com/pod-product-compliance
Lightning Source LLC
LaVergne TN
LVHW021413110826
845150LV00007B/1900
9781425510121